TWO SIDES

OF EVERY COIN

A Dialectic Formatting

of Christian Thought

James A. Fowler

C.I.Y. PUBLISHING
P.O. BOX 1822
FALLBROOK, CA 92088

TWO SIDES OF EVERY COIN

A Dialectic Formatting of Christian Thought

© 2014 by James A. Fowler

Published by C.I.Y. Publishing
P.O. Box 1822
Fallbrook, California 92088-1822

Printed in the United States of America

ISBN – 978-1-929541-53-9

DEDICATION

In the early part of the twenty-first century it was my privilege to meet and befriend a fellow Christian teacher and author by the name of Bill Freeman. In our discussions we shared the necessity of seeing both sides of every issue in Christian thought. After one such discussion he sent me a little pamphlet by Robert Govett entitled *"The Two-sidedness of Divine Truth."* Though limited in scope, the pamphlet was biblical and beneficial. Brother Bill Freeman has since graduated to glory, but I would certainly have enjoyed sharing the content of this volume with him, and I am confident that he would have enjoyed the ensuing discussion. Thank you Bill for your friendship. May you enjoy the opportunity to see all things as God sees them – for eternity!

TABLE OF CONTENTS

ADDENDA

Introduction

INTRODUCTION

The referee in his black and white uniform strides toward the center of the football field, flanked by the captains of the two opposing football teams. In the middle of the field, he reaches into his pocket and pulls out a coin, and shows the team captains which side of the coin will to be designated as "heads" and the other side as "tails." The captain of the visiting team is told to call "heads" or "tails" prior to the coin being tossed into the air. When the coin lands on the grass, they all lean over to see which side landed facing upward. If the visiting captain is correct in his call, he can make the choice of whether his team will receive the football or defer and kick the football to the other team on the initial kickoff, in anticipation of receiving the kickoff at the beginning of the second half of the game. The choice is made. The players from each team come on the field. Let the game begin!

This scenario is played out thousands of times every week during the Fall football season as youth teams, school teams (elementary, junior high, high school, college), and professional teams prepare to play their games. Each event is an example of the importance of identifying the two sides of the coin.

Not every coin has the image of a head on one side, nor the image of a tail on the other side. However, one side is always designated as the front side and the other as the backside. In the field of numismatics, those involved in the field of collecting and evaluating coins, the front side is referred to as the "obverse," and the backside as the "reverse." But whatever you call the two sides, there are two sides to every coin.

This initial illustration of flipping a coin and calling for "heads" or "tails" demonstrates an *either/or* determination of one side or the other of a coin. In Christian thought there are *either/or* contrasts of polarities and dichotomies of ideas and thoughts, that like the flipped coin will present themselves as an *either/or* wherein one side is observable and deemed important, while the other side is obstructed and/or deemed inadmissible. The problem with these *either/or* dichotomies of Christian thought is that the solution is not as clear-cut as the tossing of a coin and the outcome of an obvious "heads" or "tails." One Christian may adamantly argue that the side of the coin she has called is the only valid or viable side of the coin, while another may assert that the reverse side of the issue is the only proper and acceptable position. Both may be unwilling to consider that the other side is an acceptable expression of Christian thought.

Such has often been the interactions of Christians concerning different facets of Christian thought, leading to rancorous polemics and fracturing of doctrinal and denominational loyalties. Oh, if it were as simple as tossing a coin and exclaiming "heads" or "tails." It's just not that simple when it comes to how Christians think.

IDEOLOGICAL CONTRASTS

Most readers will be familiar with and have used Roget's *Thesaurus*. Many logophiles (those fond of words) regard Roget's *Thesaurus* as one of the three most important books ever printed in the English language (the *Bible*, Webster's *Dictionary*, and Roget's *Thesaurus*). Those three books are on my desk at all times.

Dr. Peter Mark Roget (1779-1869) was a physician, scientist, and philologist who developed the *Thesaurus* early in his life (1805), but did not publish the book until forty-seven years later (1852). His objective was not just to identify synonyms and antonyms, but he sought to build a structure of all the categories of contrasts and opposites within the English language. Modern editions of Roget's *Thesaurus* have sometimes abandoned Roget's structure to simply put the synonyms and antonyms in dictionary form, but this sacrifices the foremost value of Roget's work. Roget's original structuring of English words into contrasted classification categories is a masterpiece of thought organization and will prove valuable to all who are interested in the broad spectrum of contrasting human concepts.

By the way, the word *thesaurus* is the Greek word for "treasure," and is the word used in II Cor. 4:7 – "we have this *treasure* in earthen vessels, that the surpassing greatness of the glory may be of God and not of ourselves." What is the "treasure"? The treasure (the *thesaurus*) in our earthen vessels is Jesus Christ, who gives reality and meaning to our being. And I think it is possible to demonstrate that Jesus is the treasure that gives structure and meaning to all the contrasts of life.

Everything that exists is comprised of interactive contrastive elements – all things material and immaterial. The Triune God has the interactive persons of the Father, Son and Holy Spirit. The atoms that constitute every material thing have the interactive elements of neutrons, protons, and electrons. Not only is there such triplicity in all things, but there is also a dual element of interactivity in all things. Within God there is the opposing polarity of His transcendence in relation to His immanence; His three-ness in correlation with His oneness; His unknowability contrasted with

His knowability. In the material world we observe the dual existence of mass and motion (cf. Einstein's $E=MC^2$), the positive and negative electrical fields, the pressures of expansion and contraction, attraction and repulsion, emission and absorption. Every action has its counter-action. Roget demonstrated that in the world of human thought every concept has a contrasting opposite (ex. hot and cold, light and dark, up and down, left and right, sweet and bitter, etc.), and this is likewise true in the realm of Christian thought as we contrast God and Satan, good and evil, right and wrong, truth and error, love and selfishness, etc. (*cf. Addendum A*)

As soon as we open our Bibles to *Genesis*, to the "beginning," we begin to read of contrasts: The Uncreated God creates creation, comprised of heavens and earth. Order is formed out of disorder, as God creates light and darkness, night and day. The corporeal substance that comes from incorporeal spirit is both nonliving and living, and the living is divided into male and female, and the contrasted humans are placed into an idyllic garden where they confront two contrasting trees (the tree of life and the tree of the knowledge of the contrast between good and evil). Faced with the choice of obedience or disobedient rebellion, Adam and Eve face the consequences of life or death, and the contrasts of blessings or curses. True to life, even in the first three chapters, the Bible is replete with the counteraction of contrasts, as it is throughout.

DEFINITIONS

Before we proceed in our study of the contrasts of Christian thought, we need to consider some differing definitions. The "law of opposites" has been a phrase used in physics, philosophy, physiology, as well as morality, magic, and computers. Such terms as binary, polarity, paradox and antinomy, as well as the terms dichotomy, dialectic and dualism have been utilized in many of these disciplines of thought. We are going to briefly note some of these terms, as it is important to define and compare them. (*cf. Addendum B*)

"Binary" is a familiar term popularized in the terminology of digital computing. It means "twofold," and in digital computing refers to a mathematical "base two" usage of electronic polarity wherein two binary digits or "bits" represent short-duration pulses of low (0) and high (1) direct current voltages. In its generic definition, "binary" just means that there is two of something, and the term is used in mathematics, chemistry, music and astronomy.

"Polarity" refers to divergent "poles" of contrasting objects, actions, or ideas. It is used in electronics, nuclear fusion, philosophy and politics to represent contrasting "poles." Even psychology refers to a "bipolar disorder," wherein a person experiences the poles of ecstasy and depression, peace and panic – a manic/depressive condition. "Polarity" means there are two opposite "poles," and there are some contrasts in Christian thought that are best referred to "diametric polarities." (ex. good and evil; God and Satan; righteousness and iniquity; etc.)

"Paradox" is a term used early in Greek philosophy in the writings of Zeno of Elea. The word is derived from the Greek language: *para*=alongside and *dokein*=to appear. "Paradox" has reference to two ideas or statements that "appear alongside" of one another and appear to be contradictory or incongruous, but may contain a unifying truth when considered together. An oxymoron is a paradox reduced to two contradictory words, such as a "wise fool," or a "deafening silence."

"Antinomy" is similar to "paradox," but has to do with concepts that are "against the law" of reason (*anti*=against and *nomos*=law) because they are mutually incompatible or involve an irresolvable contradiction. Antinomies reveal the limitations of human reasoning in logical discontinuities, but do not help us to understand the contrasts.

"Dichotomy" means "to cut in two," derived from two Greek words, *dicho*=two and *timnein*=to cut. The primary meaning is that of dissection or bifurcation, and it is usually employed to refer to two opposing or contradictory subclasses without any explanation of how the two parts relate to one another. Dichotomous contrasts are often popularly identified as dualisms, but a dualism has a more technical definition.

"Dualism," simply refers to the separation or demarcation of two things from one another. In classical philosophical usage, however, it often has the specific meaning of two mutually exclusive and absolute equal forces that oppose one another and cannot be brought together, remaining in a perpetual stalemate or stand-off. The Taoist dualism of *yin/yang* is an example of such. But the Christian either/or contrast of God and Satan (*cf. Addendum A*) is not a "dualism" in this absolute and classic sense because they are not co-equal eternal forces or powers. God is the sovereign and omnipotent Almighty God, and everything and everyone else is lesser than Him and will be overcome by Him

"Dialectic" comes from a Greek word, *dialectos*, (*dia*= through and *lecto*=to talk), meaning "to speak or converse through." To talk through contrasting issues was the basis of Socratic dialogue. Plato refined the term in reference to rhetorical and forensic debate; and Aristotle used "dialectic" as the proper rules of syllogistic argumentation in formal logic. Hegel employed "dialectic" to refer to the triadic integration of thesis and antithesis in synthesis. Karl Marx's "dialectical materialism" dealt with the class struggles that bring about supposed historical progression. Kierkegaard wrote of an "inverted dialectic" that was an internal, subjective and experiential (existential) struggle of progressing towards God's objective. Karl Barth was known as a "dialectic theologian." The word "dialectic" has a long history of various meanings and requires careful definition and explanation if it is to be employed as a model for conceptual understanding.

If we wanted to "play it safe" in this present foray into philosophical theology it might be advisable to identify our study of Christian contrasts with a benign entitlement of "Christian contrarieties," thus avoiding some of the inevitable problems with semantics and evolving definitions. We will, however, go "out on a limb" to identify the contrasts as "a dialectic formatting of Christian thought," as this book is subtitled. The skepticism that many have of the word "dialectic" is no doubt due to its long and diverse history of interpretation, and thus its many varied explanations.

AN HISTORICAL SURVEY

A brief historical survey of thought contrasts and the use of the word "dialectic" with its many different interpretations of meaning will serve as a foundation for the explanation of the dialectic of complementarity that will be used in this study.

Greek thought, foundational to Western thinking, had an underlying "contrast analysis" evident from the earliest extant writings. In the mystical philosophy of Greek Orphism, the soul, regarded as the divine element in man, was considered incarcerated or entombed in the human body. Thales (623-546 B.C.), regarded as the founder of Greek philosophy, at least the Milesian school, sought to dissuade any thought of godly immanence or intervention, regarding only the tangible and material objects that could be evaluated by empirical observation to be permanent and real.

The pendulum of human thought continued to swing back and forth. Heraclitus of Ephesus (530-470 B.C.) reacted against the Milesian philosophy, positing that change was the ultimate reality, and only in the perpetual flux of constant alteration via strife and opposition could any sense of stability be achieved. His philosophy is sometimes called "fluxism."

Parmenides (c. 515-440 B.C.) reacted against the relativistic "flux theory" of Heraclitus, arguing that material things exist in themselves as part of a monistic material oneness. He argued that truth could only associated with what could be empirically verified as contrasted with the illusion of trying to conceive or anything that cannot be perceived with the sense.

Back and forth went the argumentations of the early Greek philosophers, illustrating the continuous clash of contrasting human thought, and the constant discussion of human ideas and their priority.

Socrates (c. 470-399 B.C.) focused on the art of discussion and cross-examination of contrasting ideas in order to face moral dilemmas. He believed that through the dialogue of conversational interaction in question and answer, men could derive definitions that were unequivocal in assertions that did not violate the law of non-contradiction. The objective of such interaction was to seek knowledge and do what is right, despite opposition.

Plato (c. 428-348 B.C.) was the first Greek philosopher to suggest a dialectic wherein two contrasting ideas could be unified. His "theory of ideas" was a synthesis of Heraclitus' constant flux and Parmenides' constant stasis. Whereas material things are regarded as fixed and stable, our opinions of what exists are always in flux. His contrast was between the *chora*, the material receptacle, and the "Idea." He still maintained a metaphysical factor for he regarded the "forms" and "ideas" of the intelligible world to be eternal, separating the upper world of reason and intelligence from the lower world of belief and illusory opinions.

Aristotle (384-322 B.C.), a student of Plato, while essentially an empirical materialist, focused on developing proper rules of dialogical argumentation in order to derive a logical conclusion. He formulated the syllogism of inductive logic – two premises allowing for a conclusion; the three basic rules of logic – (1) the law of identity: "whatever is, is," (2) the law of non-contradiction: "nothing can both be and not be," and (3) the law of the excluded middle: "everything must either be or not be;" and the four causes: (1) material cause –

elements out of which object is created, (2) efficient cause – means by which it is created, (3) formal cause – expression of what it is, and (4) final cause – end for which it is created (teleology).

Evidences of these previous Greek philosophies can be observed in the Gnosticism that became prevalent in the second and third centuries A.D. The dualism of the pneumatic spirit needing to be set free from the imprisonment of the body certainly has elements of Orphistic thought. In Gnostic thought the soul (or spirit) of man was regarded as divine substance, whereas the body and material world were under the malign forces of the demiurge. Through Gnostic enlightenment a person could allegedly rise above the somatic and cosmic realm into divine knowledge and participation.

Proceeding to some European thinkers, Abelard (A.D. 1079-1142) was regarded as the greatest logician of the Middle Ages. He wrote works on *Logic* and *Dialectics*, believing that the Christian faith could be rationally accounted for, but human reason alone could not be the final arbiter of the faith. The extreme rationalists he called pseudo-dialecticians, and the mystics he called anti-dialecticians, recognizing that the dialectic between God and the material world had to be maintained. His work, *Sic et Non*, literally *So and No*, was an attempt to reconcile contradictions between scripture and the church fathers.

The German priest, Nicholas of Cusa (A.D. 1401-1464), combined geometry and logic to formulate his thesis of *coincidentia oppositorum*, "the coincidence of opposites." Though the angles of a polygon are increased indefinitely, they never become a circle, and likewise man's finite attempts to explain God and His ways never adequately express the Infinite. Therefore, he concluded, the contrasting opposites in human thought must not be cast in static rigidity, but must be allowed to coincide by occupying the same space from the perspective of God's Infinity.

Several centuries later, Immanuel Kant (A.D. 1724-1804) sought to show the limitations of human logic altogether. He regarded the logic of the ancient Greek philosophers to be the "logic of illusion," arguing that formal logic could prove both the thesis and the antithesis, thus creating an antinomy of contradiction. He suggested a "transcendental dialectic" wherein transcendental knowledge, which makes all human thought possible, allows human thought to go beyond formal reason to real moral decisions that pass beyond the limits of human experience. In his *Critique of Pure Reason*, he developed a moral philosophy that advocated a categorical imperative for human experience.

Also regarding formal logic as lifeless and monotonous, Georg W. F. Hegel (A.D. 1770- 1831) explained that there is no absolute truth, but ideas evolve into more complex and truer forms within the historical mobility of human thought. Using the triadic dialectic of thesis, antithesis, and synthesis, Hegel's reductionism suggested that individual experience along with social concern would eventually lead human thought to a harmonious reconciliation of all things in the consciousness of an "absolute" awareness of the "World-Spirit." Hegel's philosophy of "absolute idealism" was the first to use "dialectic" in terms of historical change.

Though Karl Marx (A.D. 1818-1883) criticized the Hegelian dialectic of "absolute idealism," he used the dialectic of historical change as the basis of his "dialectical materialism." Using the Hegelian paradigm of thesis, antithesis, and consequent synthesis, Marx formulated the belief that sociological conflicts and class struggles over material goods would progressively liberate the oppressed and produce materialistic egalitarianism and sociological utopianism. Thesis: common ownership + poverty = primitive communalism. Antithesis: private ownership + wealth = slavery, feudalism, capitalism. Synthesis: common ownership + wealth = socialistic communism. Historical supersessionism was the driving force of his theory of "dialectical materialism."

The relatively obscure Danish philosopher, Soren Kierkegaard (A.D. 1813-1855), reacted to Hegel's theory of dialectic synthesis leading to absolute truth. He did not believe that God's absolute Truth and human thought could ever be brought together in rational synthesis, for they formed an "absolute paradox." Since God is "wholly other" than man, the need of humanity is to face the Unknown experientially and not seek to make it knowable. Because of this absolute transcendence of God from all human categories, God's revelation must be accepted by an existential or experiential "leap of faith" in the human mind. Kierkegaard is often regarded as the father of existentialist philosophy. In Kierkegaard's own words, "Christianity entered into the world not to be understood but to be existed in" ... to be lived. This cannot be expressed more strongly than by the fact that Christianity proclaims itself to be a paradox/dialectic."

Twentieth century Swiss theologian, Karl Barth (A.D. 1886-1968) appreciated Kierkegaard's thought and seems to incorporate such (at least in his early writings) in his emphasis on the radical otherness and transcendence of God compared to man. The unknowability of God by human reason (*apophatic* theology) is contrasted with the fact that God can only be known through His Self-revelation of Himself in the Son (*cataphatic* theology). What is affirmed by God in His Self-revelation (the divine "Yes") is always countered by that which is contrary to God's character and will; that which He stands against (the divine "No").

These contrasts form the basis of the designation of Barth's thought as "Dialectic Theology."

French sociologist, Jacques Ellul (A.D. 1912-1994) briefly espoused Marx's conflict theory of "dialectical materialism," but rejected such in incorporating the thought of Kierkegaard and Barth. Ellul formulated a dialectic between sociology and theology, wherein the constantly conflicted demonic powers of the fallen world are in opposition to the ultimate divine power of God revealed in the intervention of the incarnation of Jesus Christ. The necessity of technique and death in the world system is contrasted with the living freedom of the individual Christian living "in the world, but not of the world." In Ellul's words, "Dialectic, then, is not just a way of reasoning by question and answer. It is an intellectual way of grasping reality, which embraces the positive and the negatives …. It includes contradictory things that do not exclude one another, but co-exist. Hence a system of vigorous thought ought to take account of both premises without ruling out either, without choosing between, since every choice would exclude one part of reality." (Ellul, *What I Believe*, pg 31)

This brief historical review of some of the major thinkers (somewhat arbitrarily selected), and how their views of "contrast analysis" or dialectic contrasted one from the other, was necessitated to show the broad range of diversity thoughout the history of human thought. It is quite evident that different thinkers analyzed the contrasts of thought in widely divergent categories, and their reactions to prior systems of thought created more contrasts.

DIALECTIC DIVERSITY

Proceeding from the historical review, it will be instructive to compare a couple of the more modern dialectical models with the particular model that will be employed in this study. The two nineteenth century writers that have most influenced modern thought concerning dialectic are probably the German philosopher, G.W.F. Hegel, and the Danish thinker, Soren Kierkegaard. A diagrammatic comparison of their dialectic models with the model we are proposing will serve to show the differences of their approach. (*cf. Addendum C*)

Georg Hegel's dialectic of "synthetic reductionism" is constructed by juxtaposing two contrasting concepts, a "thesis" and its "antithesis," which are then merged or consolidated together into a "synthesis." (*cf. Addendum D*) The blended and consolidated "synthesis," then becomes the next "thesis" which also has an opposing dialectic "antithesis," the two of which can become joined and united into another "synthesis," and so on. This process of progressive thought compression as proposed by Hegel was considered to be the "logical science" of objective thought categories, supposed to lead to an ultimate synthesis of objective human thought which could be considered "ultimate reality," "absolute Being," or "the Mind of God," the deification of human thought processes.

There is, however, another way of evaluating Hegel's "synthetic reductionism." Instead of reaching a pinnacle of the singular "ultimate ideal," the progressive thought progression of this dialectic model could represent the "law of diminishing returns" whereby human thought is continuously boiled down to the lowest common denominator leading to the smallest grain of simplicity, able to be understood by the most challenged simpleton.

Soren Kierkegaard travelled to Germany to sit under the teaching of Georg Hegel who was regarded as the foremost thinker of his day. He did not stay long, for he rejected the objective idealism of Hegel's dialectic, opting instead for a "radical subjectivism" in the form of what he termed an "inverted dialectic." (*cf. Addendum E*).

The inversion of Kierkegaard's dialectic involves turning from objective to subjective categories, from mental ideology to personal and existential experience, and from static particulars to dynamic processes. Kierkegaard was convinced that objective mental processes alone were never going to lead human thinking to what was really true. Though his own personal relationships with other persons was as contorted as his own physical body, his philosophy proposed a personalism that countered the idealism that reigned in the popular thought of Hegel.

Arguing that "subjectivity is truth" and "truth is subjectivity," Kierkegaard maintained that the experiential circumstances of life provide the milieu in which the individual must develop subjective attitudes to deal with the absurdity of the world around him. This existential process provides the subjective dialectic of dynamic movement from sorrow to joy, from weakness to strength, from doubt to hope, from darkness to light, from death to life, from defeat to victory, and from fleshliness to godliness. Divine character coming from above in Christ and operating within an individual can supersede and overcome the meaninglessness and pain of the world we live in.

Though Kierkegaard was a committed follower of Christ, the philosophers who picked up on his existentialist philosophy of the subjective reaction to the absurdity and despair of the world were mostly humanistic and atheistic. Examples include Friedrich Nietzsche, Jean-Paul Sartre, and Albert Camus. It must be noted, however, that Christian thinkers such as Swiss theologian Karl Barth and French sociologist Jacques Ellul also owed much of the background of their dialectic thinking to Kierkegaard.

With these two diverse illustrative models in mind, we must now address the interactive dialectics proposed in this study. To illustrate this model of dialectic thought (*cf. Addendum F*), we commence with the divine pivot point of God's Self-revelation whereby all truth is known. This divine reality of divine Being, character, and revelation provides the stationary hinge for all human thinking. Contrary to Hegel's objective ideal to be sought by human dialectic thinking and designated as the ultimate (god), and contrary to Kierkegaard's subjective positing of an introspective awareness of God revealed Christologically and experienced existentially, this dialectic model hangs everything on the revelatory hinge of God in Christ and the written record of such in the inspired scriptures.

From the divine pivot point of God's revelation we discover numerous (perhaps innumerable) *both/and* themes, topics, tenets, and theses that form dynamic dialectics – what Nicolas of Cusa called *coincidentia oppositorum.* They may appear to be opposites, but they are not to be viewed as a contradictory paradox, an irrational antinomy, or even as the Hegelian contrast of thesis and antithesis. These two statements or concepts, both consistent with God's revelation, must be regarded as truths that complement one another, rather than compete with one another seeking to negate the other. Consistent with the etymological meaning of "dialectic," these two tenets must "talk through" and dialogue with each other in a continual conversation of dynamic reciprocity that maintains a tensioned balance of the two thoughts.

These two ideas, concepts, or truth-statements serve as a counter-balance to each other, similar to the musical counterpoint where voices are dependent from one another while also interdependent upon the other for a complete expression. It will be observed that these contrasting dialectic tenets often juxtapose objective and subjective conceptual categories, and thus serve to balance Hegelian objectivity and Kierkegaardian subjectivity in a balanced perspective of God's revealed truth.

As the pendulum of thought swings back and forth between these contrasting themes, note that the failure to maintain a tensioned balance of dialectic complementarity of the two concepts simultaneously results in a one-sided interpretation that is an extremist aberration of the fullness of divine perspective. The ...isms of man-made human thought, so evident in religious argumentation, are usually the result of denying, diminishing or neglecting one premise, or placing undue importance and dominance on one tenet over the other. (*cf. Addendum G*)

The *both/and* of the complementary dialectic soon becomes an *either/or* of dichotomous polarity when the extremes of one-sided interpretations collide in conflict with each other. Convinced that their one-sided interpretation is the absolute truth of proper and acceptable thought, they take sides across the chasm of misunderstanding, regarding their interpretation to be "right," and the other "wrong." Then, contrary to dialectic, the two sides engage in the *antilectic* of talking against one another in agitated debate and polemics.

Despite the possibility of the contested and extremist *either/or* positions, this model of a dialectic of interactive complementarity of contrasted *both/and* concepts certainly seems preferable over Hegel's dialectic reductionism and Kierkegaard's dialectic existentialism. Hanging, as it does, on the pivot point of divine revelation, this dialectic allows for the dynamic interchange and interplay of differing conceptual ideas that should lead to balanced human thinking and harmonious relations between those with differing opinions.

ELUCIDATION OF
INTERACTIVE DIALECTICS

The tensioned interactivity of the *both/and* dialectic runs counter to the western mind-set that is based on an Aristotelian paradigm of linear logic and closed-ended conclusions. Aristotle's laws of human logic included the "law of non-contradiction," indicating that if two truths were opposite of one another, then they could not both be true, for truth cannot be contradictory. Coinciding with the "law of non-contradiction was the "law of the excluded middle," indicating that genuine opposites could not allow for a middle-ground between the two, for they are diametrically opposed to each other with no common ground. (Hegel apparently disregarded the rule of the excluded middle in his proposed synthesis of thesis and antithesis).

So, it must be admitted that the *both/and* interactive dialectic model being proposed in this study is counterintuitive to the western mind-set and way of thinking. Should that concern a Western Christian thinker? Not necessarily! The prophet, speaking on behalf of God said, "My thoughts are not your thoughts, neither are your ways My ways, ... For as the heavens are higher than the earth, so are My ways higher than your ways, and My thoughts than your thoughts" (Isa. 55:8,9). The apostle Paul exclaimed, "Oh, the depths of the riches both of the wisdom and knowledge of God! How unsearchable are His judgments and unfathomable are His ways!" (Rom. 11:33). To the Corinthians, Paul wrote, "Has not God made foolish the wisdom of the world? For since in the wisdom of God the world through its wisdom did not *come to* know God. ... The foolishness of God is wiser than men, and the weakness of God is stronger than men" (I Cor. 1:21,24). God's wisdom and God's ways cannot be enveloped within or confined to finite Western thought patterns.

It is incumbent upon Western Christian thinkers to "think outside of the box" of their culturally accustomed postulates of finite human reasoning, and beyond the particular theological persuasions wherein they have found refuge. The "mystery" of divine revelation cannot be contained in static humanly-crafted thought boxes. The *either/or* paradigm of Western thought must give way to an expansive and comprehensive *both/and* consideration of the revealed mystery of Theologic and divine perspective.

One respondent objected to the *both/and* dialectic model proposed in this study, calling it a "horrid tool of the devil." Another denied that there could be "opposing truths," stating, "It is impossible to avoid going around in circles with people that believe in two opposing realities. They literally believe one thing and its opposite, so it is entirely impossible to resolve a matter." What can one say to persons who are so entrenched in their Western thought patterns? Perhaps one could say, "It is impossible to convince a person that there are two sides of a coin, when the person adamantly insists and persists in looking at only one side. It reveals a one-dimensional perspective!"

We began this study by noting that there are two sides to every coin, and the two sides are popularly referred to as either "heads" or "tails." Though a human observer cannot see both sides of a coin at the same time that does not mean that both sides of the coin do not exist simultaneously. Our human eyes, positioned as they are by divine creation, both look forward and cannot view both sides of the same coin at the same time. It might be possible, however, to place two mirrors at a ninety-degree angle to each other, placing a coin vertically between the two mirrors, and thus viewing both sides of the coin in the reflection of the mirrors. That would allow us to see two reflections of the same coin simultaneously, but technically not both sides of the same coin directly at the same time.

Such is the difficulty that our finite minds seem to have in viewing two contrasting ideas, concepts, tenets, or positions at the same time, and accepting that they have a "common ground" of veracity requiring that they be viewed, accepted and maintained in a mutual counterbalance. The objective is not to attempt to determine if one is more valid or accurate than the other, or if one supersedes or takes priority over the other, but to see them stereoscopically at the same time, to see each truth together with the other synoptically. Someone might object by asking, "But how can you see double without being double-minded?" Did not James indicate, "a double minded man is unstable in all his ways" (James 1:8)? The synchronous and simultaneous mental observation of two postulates does not make a person double-minded, anymore than viewing an object with two eyes that form a common focal point creates double-vision in human sight.

Many Western Christian thinkers are afraid of the "dialectic reciprocity" of the *both/and* categories. They are fearful that the dynamic interaction of seemingly contradictory concepts allows for a "wishy-washy," unstable, hypocritical, or even bipolar form of Christian thinking – perhaps even double-entendre mind-games whereby one is allowed to speak out of both sides of one's mouth. There is a collective paranoia about the inter-related themes of *both/and* contrasts.

Some have even charged that a *both/and* dialectic that maintains two tenets simultaneously is a form of relativism that is unwilling to formulate absolutes. Is it our objective in Christian thought to formulate rigid, air-right propositional absolutes of information? Or are we willing to see that God is the divine and personal Absolute who has revealed His wisdom and His ways in contrasting themes that require counterbalancing interaction that allows each to interpret the other?

How difficult it seems to be for many Western thinkers to accept a synoptic perspective of synchronistic mutuality of contrasting ideas. Wanting everything absolutized in precise systematic explanations of ideological certainty, Western thinkers either try to synthesize the two concepts in Hegelian reductionism, or emphasize one premise to the neglect, diminishment, denial, or exclusion of the other in a one-sided extremism.

Western Christian thinkers tend to eschew the counter-tension of *both/and* dialectic thinking. They are uncomfortable with the indefinite tension of contrasts, and often attempt to take one premise and elevate it to supremacy over the other. Regarding this idea to be the "whole" of the truth of the matter, they eschew and repudiate the other premise. They seek to dissect the premises of a *both/and* contrast and push them out into *either/or* polarities, with absolute definition in the defined "absolutes" of their particular belief-system.

The diagrams that we will be using in this study to illustrate the over-emphasis of one tenet or the other employ columns on each side representing the aberrant extremisms that result from such one-dimensional thinking that fails to maintain the dialectic tension. These might be represented as the thought-ditches that one tends to slide into when one veers off of the dual-lane road of the dialectic being considered.

AVOIDING THE DITCHES

As we consider these various dialectics and the ditches that we can so easily slide into if we fail to maintain balanced thinking, we will all realize that we have slid into a few ditches in our thought processes. As the study progresses, we may find ourselves crawling out of a few ditches along the way, not wanting to get stuck in the muddy muck and mire of misinformed thinking. (*cf. Addenda H*)

In fact, some of us have had so much difficulty staying on the two-lane road in some of these categories, that we may have been like a drunk, swerving from ditch to ditch – in and out of one and then into another. A balanced sense of sober perspective is difficult to maintain in some of these areas of thought on the Christian journey. Especially since religion seems to advocate that the safest place, in order to maintain a straight course, is to ride in one ditch or the other: "Follow the ditch-course; it's far less risky that swerving back and forth on the unmarked dialectic highway."

When I was learning to drive on the rural dirt roads of south-central Kansas in the mid-1960s, our driver's education instructor informed us that the best way to drive the muddy country roads was to "stay in the double ruts, where you were less likely to slide into the ditches." It worked most of the time, although I found myself in the ditch on several occasions (one time with a school bus full of children). The advice of the driver's education instructor has some pertinence for traveling the roads of dialectic thought. "Keep your wheels in the double channels of the dialectic, where you will be less likely to slide into the ditches."

As we consider some dialectics of Christian thought do not be surprised when you discover that you have been (or perhaps presently are) traveling in a ditch, or maybe just steering and veering very close to a ditch. Do not fret; we have all been stuck a few times in a ditch, and the purpose of this study is to consider how to stay the course of balanced Christian thought.

ILLUSTRATING THE BOTH/AND DYNAMIC

My mind has always sought to find reasonable balance. In my personal office I do not have religious icons or other such "holy hardware." Instead, I have a row of balance scales, and on another wall a bronze statue of the blind-folded Roman goddess, Lady Justice (Latin *Iustitia*), aka the Greek goddess *Themis* or *Dike*, holding a balance scale. More than one person has entered my office and asked if I was a lawyer. "No," I respond, "I just seek balance in every category of human thought.

But the balance scale is an inadequate illustration for the dialectic we are considering because it is a static balance. The *both/and* dialectic being proposed in this study is more like a pendulum that involves a dynamic motion from side to side. Another example of dynamic balance can be seen in the exercise of learning to ride a bicycle. It is very difficult to balance a bicycle when it is static and not moving, but when there is forward motion the rider finds it easier to learn how to turn left and right to maintain dynamic balance.

My wife and I have four daughters who were all competitive gymnasts when they were young. The balance beam is perhaps the most difficult apparatus in women's gymnastics. On a four-inch wide leather-covered sixteen foot beam, four feet above the ground, the female gymnast performs stunts that require precise dynamic balance. It was the event where we as parents held our breath until the routine was completed.

Jean-Paul Sartre, a secular existentialist dialectician, likened the dynamic action of a dialectic to a woman's "wiggling bottom." There is no attempt to be sexist here, but a woman's anatomy seems to better illustrate the point. It's just the way God made them! Watching a walking woman from the backside, her posterior portion wiggles back and forth. It is not static, but quite dynamic. And the point being made here is that a *both/and* dialectic involves a reciprocity that goes from side to side, back and forth.

Perhaps the best illustration is that of a tree swing. We had a large pine tree in the backyard of our home. Placing two lengths of chain over a horizontal tree limb, I constructed a tree swing. This illustration is particularly apt since the pivot point for the swing is at the top, as in the both/and dialectic that we are proposing. The grandchildren were not content with the static equilibrium of just sitting on the seat while the ropes hung from the tree. They wanted the dynamic motion of swinging back and forth ... back and forth ... back and forth ... in a reciprocal action. They did not seem to tire of it. They were constantly hollering, "Push me again Papa ... higher ... harder ... faster ... again ..."

Just as the grandchildren were not content to sit on the seat and hang from the tree in the "dead center" position of the swing, neither should we be concerned or content with seeking a "dead center" synthesis or fusion of the two concepts of a *both/and* dialectic. We are not even concerned with attempting to develop a "middle" position of consensus or agreement between the two positions, wherein they "meet half way." We only want to accept the full "posits" of the two positions, and maintain them both in a balanced tension, allowing neither to diminish the other, or to swallow up the other in any way.

An interactive dialectic accepts the dynamic interplay of the two concepts, as they bounce off of each other and provide definition, clarification, and limitation to each other in so doing. To the sounds of a syncopated counterpoint, the two concepts "dance around in the same space" perichoretically. The *both/and* conceptual contrasts are not meant to *compete* with each other, but to *complete* each other in a dynamic complimentarity. In the back-and-forth balanced tension of dialectic reciprocity the two themes provide explication of the fullness of the Divine Mystery in a manner that cannot be fully explained in singular postulates of finite reasoning within an *either/or* paradigm.

PHILOSOPHICAL DIALECTIC
OF "BEING" AND "DOING"

To set up the *both/and* dialectic charts prepared for this study, it will be helpful to go back to early Greek philosophical thought and consider what may be the foundational dialectic of human thinking. We are going to call it the *both/and* dialectic of "being" and "doing" (a.k.a. "essence" in contrast to "function"). In so doing we attempt to connect the history of human thought through the centuries to the initial dialectic charts that we will be employing.

In the classical Greek philosophers, whose thought underlies Western thought patterns, we can see that Plato and Aristotle seem to have an *either/or* distinction in their thought and methodology, which need not remain as a dichotomy, but can be formulated as a *both/and* dialectic. That is one of the epiphenomenal traits of dialectic thought; an *either/or* dichotomy can become a *both/and* dialectic when viewed in another context.

One of the supreme objectives of the classical Greek thinkers was to describe and define "Being" (*cf. Addendum I*). They searched for and sought to articulate the "ideal idea" that was the supreme and real essence of "being" – the "really real," the ultimate IS, the supreme substance, the universal Mind, the One (Tὸ Ἔν) Reality behind everything.

Plato used the *a priori* method of deductive logic whereby he posited and projected a singular ultimate "Being" (not necessarily personal) that constituted the essential essence of all that IS. This is not unlike Einstein's search for the "unified field theory" that would explain all the workings of the universe!

But Plato's pupil, Aristotle, was actually more in line with the methodology of Einstein, utilizing the *a posteriori* method of inductive logic whereby he sought to work backwards from what was observable evidence, to then explain the essential "Being" intrinsic to all that exists. In Aristotle's approach the expressed result of the "doing" or outcome of the "being" was regarded as a means to lead human thought back to a more accurate explanation of the "Being." The observable evidence of the expression should lead to an understanding of the essence! This is the basis of what we call "the scientific method" today.

These classical methodological approaches for the acquisition of human knowledge have long been recognized as complementary parallel processes for a balanced *both/and* dialectic approach to human understanding. Deductive and inductive logical approaches both have their place in human reasoning.

Throughout the history of human thought it can be demonstrated how the categories of "being" and "doing" seem to be present time and again. Moving from Plato and Aristotle, we can proceed to the history or Christian theology by noting the contrasting approaches of Augustine, a neo-Platonist who approached Christian thought by postulating the "Being" of God in superlative substantialist categories, which can be and contrasted with Thomas Aquinas, who utilized the Aristotelian approach of emphasizing the evidentiary "doing" side of the couplet in order to articulate his "proofs" for the existence of the "Being" of God.

By the time we move to the German philosophers of the eighteenth and nineteenth centuries, we find Georg Wilhelm Friedrich Hegel advocating objective logical dialectics of "being" in logical categories which can be synthesized (thesis, antithesis, synthesis). This was countered, for example, by the Danish philosopher-thinker, Soren Kierkegaard, who emphasized a subjective inverted dialectic that dealt with the experiential, personal and existential, and advocated that "being" was grounded in active relationality and personalism.

The interactive dialectic of recognizing both "being" and "doing" finds its origin in the contrast between Plato and Aristotle, but the philosophical foundations of these early thinkers must be applied to Christian categories. (cf. Addendum J)

The both/and interactive dialectics in the charts that follow represent the patterning by which I have formatted my thinking for the past twenty years. I have learned much from Kierkegaard and Barth, but my dialectical thinking was most influenced by the writings of the French thinker, Jacques Ellul, who was himself influenced by Kierkegaard and Barth. Since the early 1990s, when I first read Ellul's writings, I have been jotting down contrastual *both/and* dialectic charts whenever they come to mind (often in the early hours of the morning when I am awakening). As I began to prepare for this study, I found over five hundred pages of dialectic rough drafts filed under "dialectics."

These dialectic charts are just the skeletal scaffolding of a comprehensive dialectic theology. They need to be filled in and fleshed out with more comprehensive explanation of each topic. That would create a massive volume of a very different kind of theology than is usually found in the academic theological textbooks. It would comprise a new paradigm of considering theology from a balanced dialectical format.

Interactive

Both/And Dialectics:

Historic Contrast

of Being and Doing

GOD

Dialectic – Both/And

← Extremism	BEING	DOING	Extremism →
Classic Theism - Platonism	Essence - IS	Energies, activity - DO	**Pelagianism**
Substantialism - Attempting to determine God's Being as a composite of substantive concepts, ideas, or attributes.	Intrinsic Being - *a se* - in and of Himself. God IS who He IS, autonomously and independent of any other. God's BEING is not established by His DOING	Self-generating action *ek autos* - out of Himself God DOES what He DOES because He IS who He IS. - never contingent on any one or anything else to function as He functions.	**Arminianism?** **Humanism** - posits that God's action is contingent on human action. **Charismatics** - sometimes indicate that God's action requires a supernatural display.
Augustinianism - Neoplatonic reversion to substantialist categories of determining and explaining God's Being.	God's Being is understood in a Christian perspective only by the dynamic relationality of Father, Son, and Holy Spirit.	God's Self-revelation in the Son, Jesus Christ, informs our understanding of the relationality of God's Being.	**Defining God's BEING on basis of His DOING;** ie. God is loving, thus God is Love, then God is but logical product of His own action.
	God's BEING is fixed in absoluteness and eternality - immutable. His BEING who He IS, ie. LOVE, necessitates His DOING for others.	God's active DOING is always permeated and empowered by the presence of His BEING. - God does not act at a distance by virtual reality.	

God

Dialectic – Both/And

Extremism →

Being	Doing
Divine Being of God What God *is* only God *is*.	God *does* what He *does*, because He *is* Who He *is*.
Isa. 46:9 - "No one like Me" Deut. 6:4 - "Lord is one" Ps. 97:9 - "exalted far above all gods" Ps. 90:2 - "from everlasting to everlasting You are God Exod. 3:14 - "I AM...I AM" Jn. 10:30 - "I and the Father are one" I Tim. 1:17 - "King eternal, immortal, invisible..." I Cor. 1:9 - "God is faithful" Isa. 43:7 - "everything created for My glory" Gen. 17:1 - "God Almighty" I Pet. 1:16 - "I am holy" I Jn. 4:8,16 - "God is love" – **"Ontological**	Heb. 12:23 - "Judge of all" Ps. 115:3 - "He does what He pleases" (always in accord with His character) Jn. 3:16 - "God so loved the world that He gave Son" II Tim. 1:9,10 - "purpose and grace revealed by the appearing of the Savior" Eph. 3:11 - "purpose carried out in Jesus Christ" Rom. 5:5 - "love of God poured out by Holy Spirit" James 1:17 - "every good & perfect gift from above" II Tim. 1:9 - "grace granted to us in Christ Jesus" **Dynamic"** – **GRACE**

Extremism →

Dynamism

Operationalism

Ontologism

Essentialism

God

Dialectic – Both/And

Extremism	Being	Doing	Extremism
Substantialism Rationalism	Greek perspective: - Logically reasoned and conjectured attributes of a speculative supreme superlative.	Greek perspective: - Superlative so far removed from matter, there is no "doing" that relates to the world.	Dualism Gnosticism
Deism Favoritism Nationalism	Hebrew perspective: - Elevated supercessory Almighty Being who expected faithful nation of ethnic people.	Hebrew perspective: - God imposed legal covenant arrangements, yet remained contained in ark, tabernacle, temple.	Legalism Behaviorism "God in the box"
Determinism Rationalism - God can be figured out	Reformed perspective: - Deterministic personal Being whose immutable and consistent ways can be systematized.	Reformed perspective: - God acts sovereignly to implement His predetermined, proceduralized Plan and ways.	Particularism Arbitrary imposition
Unjustifiable mercy	Grace perspective: - God of constant, unending love has reached out to mankind in the incarnation of His Son, to redemptively restore men.	Grace perspective: - God's grace action is always via the Son by the Spirit to freely express His relational love uniquely to receptive individuals.	Universalism Personalism

49

Satan

Dialectic – Both/And

Being	Doing
Extrinsic and derivative being of the Evil One. - began as derivative creature, spirit-being, with freedom of choice to rebel and refuse intended purpose as Lucifer (light-bearer).	Derivative activity - A derivative creature cannot self-generate character: - not godly character - not character contrary to the character of God.
The derivative Being of the Evil One, with character contrary to the character of God is the conundrum of theodicy.	How then does the Evil One tempt individuals to express evil character, and thus to sin against the character of God?
Evil - Jn. 17:15; II Th. 3:3 Sinful - I Jn. 3:8 Liar - Jn. 8:44; Acts 5:3 Murderer - I Jn. 3:12 Deceiver - Rev. 12:9; 20:2 Self-exalting - Isa. 14:14	enslaves - II Tim 2:26 blinds minds - II Cor 4:4 death-dealer - Heb. 2:14 sin-source - I Jn. 3:8,10,12 tempts - I Th. 3:5; I Cor 7:5 accuses - Rev. 12:10 hinders - I Th. 2:18

Must avoid positing a dualism wherein the being of God and Satan are equal and neither is supreme over the other.

Neither do we discount or deny the "being" of Satan as an imaginative myth or metaphorical personification.

God and Satan are not in a dualistic stalemate of power or ability whereby one cannot overcome the other.

Satan's power has been overcome by the person and work of Jesus Christ, and Christians need not cower in fear of the devil.

Humanity

Dialectic – Both/And

Extremism	Being	Doing	Extremism
Humanism - indicates that the being of humanity is independent and autonomous, thus positing the deification of humanity. Monism Panentheism - humans are essentially one with spirit-forces.	Human being is extrinsic being. We did not create ourselves. Our being is derived from another – from the Creator God. Spiritual condition of "being" is derived from indwelling presence and function of spirit-person. Spiritual nature of individual is the nature of the spiritual personage (God or Satan) who indwells him/her. Fall of man, with spiritual usurpation of Satan over/in mankind, necessitated divine restoration of man.	Humans are not little gods who are self-generative of their own character or activity. They are dependent and derivative. This necessitates recognition that human beings are choosing creatures having freedom of choice to make determinative decisions of receptivity. - Faith is our receptivity of God's activity. II Cor. 3:5 - "not adequate to consider anything as coming from ourselves" Jn. 15:5 - "Apart from Me you can do nothing"	Humanism - implies that human initiative and potential are intrinsic ability of mankind. - human "doing" determines human "being" of self-identity. "I am what I do" Pelagianism – (religious humanism) - indicates that human choice creates a necessary contingency that forces God to act.

Jesus Christ

Dialectic – Both/And

← Extremism

Being	Doing
The hypostatic union of Jesus establishes His being as fully God and fully man. It is not unthinkable that the Messianic Savior could *be* God and *be* man at the same time.	The function of God and man, i.e. Self-generative vs. derived, are incapable of simultaneity. Jesus could not *behave* as God and *behave* as man at the same time.
Intrinsic Being (God) and extrinsic being (man) could be conjoined in the unique being of a divine-human God-man.	The Son of God emptied Himself (Phil. 2:7) of the prerogative of divine function in order to function as derivative man.
"The Word was made flesh" (Jn. 14:10). "being made in the likeness of man, ...in appearance as a man" (Phil. 2:7,8).	"I do nothing of My own initiative; the Father abiding in Me does His works" (cf. Jn. 5: 30; 8:28:42; 12:49; 14:10)

Extremism →

Left (Being) Extremism:

Evangelical Calvinism - attempts to extend the hypostatic union to encompass the entirety of humanity, utilizing the theological novelty of the "vicarious humanity" of Jesus Christ to indicate the replacement of all sinful humanness in the person and work of Jesus.

Right (Doing) Extremism:

Evangelicalism - employs apologetic arguments attempting to prove the deity of Jesus by the functionality of His "doing." - ex. miracles are alleged to prove deity of Christ

Misinterpreted kenoticism

Passivism

Holy Spirit

Dialectic – Both/And

← Extremism

→ Extremism

Being	Doing
Relational Person within the Divine Being of the Triune Godhead.	Acts only by the Divine dynamic of the grace of the Triune God.

• Spirit of God
  - Rom. 8:9 - "Spirit of God dwells in you"
• Spirit of Christ
  - Rom. 8:9 - "If any man does not have Spirit of Christ, he is none of His"
• Holy Spirit
  - Rom. 5:5 - "Holy Spirit has been given to us".
	• Life-giving Spirit
	  - I Cor. 15:45 - "Last Adam became life-giving Spirit"
	• Pours out Love of God
	  - Rom. 5:5 - "love of God poured into our hearts by Holy Spirit"
	• Glorifies Christ
	  - Jn. 16:14 - "glorify Me"

Fruit of the Spirit -divine character is: "love, joy, peace, patience, kindness, goodness, faithfulness, gentleness, self-control" (Gal. 5:22,23)	Gifts of the Spirit -ministry within the Body of Christ, the Church, is accomplished by the activity of the Holy Spirit via the spiritual giftedness of Christian peoples.

Extremism (Being):

Academic understanding of the Holy Spirit as "third person of the Godhead."

Misunderstanding that "fruit" is produced by human effort of evangelism or behavior performance.

Extremism (Doing):

Elevation of admiration for the action of the Holy Spirit, even above the divine Father and Son.

Pentecostalism

Charismaticism

Supernaturalism

Christian

Dialectic – Both/And

Being | Doing

← Extremism (Being side) | Extremism → (Doing side)

	Being	Doing
	As all human "being" is extrinsic being and derived being, the Christian has spiritually exchanged the derivation of spiritual "being" (*exousia*) from Satan to God (Acts 26:18) in spiritual regeneration.	As all functional expression of character and behavior in what humans do is derived from spiritual source, the activity of Christian behavior is expressive of the character of God or Satan.
	The contrast of this spiritual condition of "being:" death ... life darkness ... light natural ... spiritual child of devil ... child of God wrath nature ... divine nature iniquity ... righteousness sinner ... saint	The contrast of this behavior is explained by the conflict of the impetus of the "flesh" or the "Spirit" in Christian's behavior. - deeds of the flesh (Gal. 5:19-21) - fruit of the Spirit (Gal. 5:22,23)

Humanism (Being extremism)
- A human's being is intrinsic to him/her self.
- For this reason every person is encouraged to "be all you can be!" "You can be anything you set your mind to be."

Humanism (Doing extremism)
- Human activity is regarded to be self-generative, so every person is encouraged to perform to the best of their ability, "for your success and destiny is entirely up to you."

Religious Humanism
- most religion is humanistic God-talk.

Church

Dialectic – Both/And

Extremism ←	**Being**	**Doing**	→ Extremism
Ecclesiasticism Institutionalism	Nature of the Church	Mission of the Church	Programs Techniquism
Perceptions of the Church as a building - or as a denomi-national entity - or as public services of in-vigoration, edu-cation, or enter-tainment.	The "being" of the Church is the Person of the living Lord Jesus dwelling in Christians collectively.	The Church is called to "do"/express the ministry of Christ via giftedness of the Spirit.	Evangelical Humanism
	The "being" of the Church is defined in the desig-nation of "the Body of Christ." (cf. Rom. 12:2; 1 Cor. 12:27; Eph. 3:6; 4:12)	"Apart from Me you can *do* nothing" (Jn. 15:5)	Performance advocacy - commitment - dedication - consecration
Church conceived as "membership" in organization - "joining the church"	This Body is likened to a living organism of which every Christian is to be a functional member. (cf. Rom. 12:4,5; I Cor. 12:12-27; Eph. 5:30)	"it is God who is at work in you, both to will and to *do* for His good pleasure" (Phil. 2:13) "May God ... equip you in every good thing to *do* His will, working in us that which is pleasing in His sight" (Heb. 13:21)	"Works" - "do this, do that" - "working for Jesus" - must serve Jesus (cf. Acts 17:25

Interactive

Both/And Dialectics

within Christian

Doctrinal Thought

Trinitarian Monotheism

Dialectic – Both/And

← Extremism | One Being | Three Persons | Extremism →

Extremism	One Being	Three Persons	Extremism
Mathematical oneness - single integer of one.	Unity, simplicity, singular	Multiple, plural, complex, distinction	Tritheism - 3 gods polytheism
• Monadic monotheism: - Jehovah (Jewish) - Allah (Islam) unextended unit of one. • Monistic monotheism - singular god extended into all things.	One supreme God: Deut. 6:4; Mk. 12:29; I Cor. 8:6; Eph. 4:6; I Tim. 2:5.	Father, Son, Holy Spirit co-equal, co-essential, co-eternal.	Misunderstanding of threeness: • Subordination-ism – Son & Spirit subordinated to Father like 2nd-class citizens. • Arianism - Son and Spirit inferior demi-gods.
	Monotheism - one essence, nature and being. Council of Nicea (A.D.325) Plurality of persons are essentially & consubstantially the same Being - *homoousion*.	Jn. 10:30 - "I and the Father are one." Jewish leaders considered this to be blasphemy. Christian obliged to explain Trinity.	*anomoousion* - not same being. *heteroousion* - different beings *homoiousion* - like, similar being
Unitarianism	Gregory of Nazianzus *perichoresis* - coinherence and interpenetration of the distinct triune persons. Jn. 14:10,11 - "I am in the Father, and the Father is in Me."	Tertullian - used Latin *trinitas* - triunity. Council of Nicea (AD 325) Greek - *hypostases* 3 particulars, persons Latin - *personae* 3 persons	• Modalism

GOD

Dialectic – Both/And

Extremism	Supremely Intentional	Self-limited	Extremism
Augustinianism	Free-will of God — free to determine action in accord w/ character. — power to implement the action He determines.	Can anyone limit God? God can Self-limit Himself God determined to Self-limit His action toward mankind, to allow human freedom of choice to enter into loving personal relationship by receptivity of faith.	Pelagianism
Calvinism	Predestination - God pre-horizoned that His action with mankind would be via His Son, Jesus Christ. (cf. 1 Cor. 2:7; Eph. 1:5)	God is relationally Triune. — He desires faith/love relationship with human creatures.	Arminianism
Reformed theology	— Jesus - "sum of all spiritual things" (Eph. 1 Election - Jesus is the Elect One; those in Christ are the "elect of God"	— He does not impose His will, purpose, desires, love, grace, upon humans	Humanism
Divine determinism	Purposes of God – Eph. 3:11- "eternal purpose carried out in Jesus"	God is always FOR us; not against us!	Individualism
Absolutism	The Almighty God, superior above all is all-powerful to implement His intentions.	Mankind has freedom of choice to receive God's intentions in Jesus Christ	Human potential. "Man makes it happen."
Fatalism			God's actions are contingent on human actions.
Arbitrary imposition of God's intentions.			The "elect" are those who select.
Misuse of term "sovereignty" in reference to God.			Irrelevancy of God's intentions.
Irrelevancy of human choices.			

GOD

Dialectic – Both/And

Extremism	Creator	Sustainer	Extremism
Deism - the non-interference and non-intervention of God in the world He has created. - the world runs solely by "the laws of nature." "God wound up the world like a clock, and sits back at a distance to observe how it runs."	Almighty, omnipotent God has brought all other things into being. - without necessity - *ek Theos; ex Deo* Gen. 1:1 - "God created the heavens and the earth" Job 33:4 - "the Spirit of God has made me" Isa. 45:7 - "One forming light ... creating darkness" Jn. 1:3 - "apart from Him nothing came into being" Col. 1:16 - "by Him all things were created... through Him & for Him" Heb. 11:3 - "worlds were prepared by word of God"	God wills and provides for continued existence and function of created order. - providential preserves - continued relationship Ps. 119:116 - "Sustain me according to Your word" Heb. 1:3 - "He upholds all things by the word of His power." Col. 1:17 - "in Him all things hold together" Creation dependent, contingent, derives from God for sustainability. Requires divine freedom to interact with creation as relational God.	Pantheism Monism - Created order sustained by the intrinsic presence of the divine comprising the essence of the material order. Anthropic Cosmological Principle. - Humanity sustains creation - ex. counters "global warming"

God's Presence

Dialectic – Both/And

← Extremism (Transcendent)	Transcendent	Immanent	Extremism (Immanent) →
Deism - distant, removed, separated.	God above and beyond His creation, beyond space & time. In a class by Himself:	God involved in & present in space/time creation. Nearness, closeness of God	Pantheism Monism Immanentism Mysticism
God regarded as "wholly other" - "out there, up there"	Independent, autonomous Self-sufficient, Sovereign Infinite qualitative difference - God and man.	• In creation - omnipresent Col. 1:17 - "In Him all things consist" Ps. 139:7 - "where can I flee from Your presence"	God is indistinguishable from the created order. - evil impossible
God not in control of universe He created.	I Chron. 29:11 - "Yours is the dominion, O God" Ps. 113:5 - "our God enthroned on high" Isa. 57:15 - "high and exalted One" Jere. 23:23 - "a God who is near...and a God far off"	• In new creation Jn. 1:14 - "Word became flesh" - incarnation Col. 1:27 - "Christ in you" I Cor. 6:17 - "one spirit with Him" - union I Jn. 4:12,15,16 - "God abides in us" Gal. 4:6 - "Spirit of His Son in our hearts"	Humanization of God. Man becomes god or a God
Gnosticism - God cannot come into contact with that which is lesser than His spiritual reality.	God is worthy subject of awe, reverence, worship.		Over-familiarization with God. - "God is my buddy"

62

GOD

Dialectic – Both/And

Extremism	UNCHANGEABLE	CHANGEABLE	Extremism
Fixed invariability of God - rigid, inflexible.	Immutable - unchanging, fixed.	Mutable - able to change, flexible	Open Theism / Process Theology
Determinism Augustinian-Calvinism, Reformed	Essential Being Sacrosanct constancy - consistent faithfulness	Divine Activity - Doing Divine freedom to choose course of action	God is Becoming - Evolving God
God is predictable Can be figured out - Proceduralized into unchanging principles - static, mechanical.	God is "the same yesterday, today, and forever" - Heb. 13:8	God can repent, relent, & accomodate Himself II Kings 20:5; Ps. 106:45; Jere. 26:3; 42:10	Divine relativism
	"I, the Lord, do not change" - Malachi 3:6		God is fickle - unpredictable and variable
God is perfect - perfect does not change.	"The Lord will not change His mind" - Ps. 110:4	Response to prayer - Exod. 32:9-14 Incarnation - New covenant (Jere. 31:31; Heb. 8:8,13	Conditionalism - our choices and actions change God and His activity.
Denial that God could Self-limit Himself without ceasing to be God.	"Father of lights ... no variation or shifting shadow" James 1:17	God is novel in every Christian's life.	Does this impinge on faithfulness of God?

GOD

Dialectic – Both/And

Extremism → | Extremism →

UNKNOWABLE	KNOWABLE
Apophatic / Anaphatic *apo*=apart from *phemi*=to speak The incommunicable, hidden God.	Kataphatic Theology *kata*=according to *phemi*=to speak The revealed God.
God is infinite - Finite mind of man can't comprehend. Inexplicable. God is eternal. - Temporal time/space perspective of man.	God can only be known as He reveals Himself. God revealed Himself in the Son, Jesus Christ. - not truth propositions of scripture.
Job 11:7 - "can you discover the depths of God?" Rom. 11:33 - "the depths of the knowledge of God" I Cor. 2:9 - "the thoughts of God no one knows"	Jn. 14:7 - "If you've known Me, you've known Father" Jn. 17:3 - "eternal life, that they know You..." If Jesus is God, then God is knowable!
Mystery of God - ineffable God cannot be known "in Himself," essential Being.	Experiential, relational knowing of God in Christ. -illuminating of Holy Spirit EOC - experience energies of God

Extremism (Unknowable):

Deism
- detach, inaccessibility of God

Since God is an unthinkable and incomprehensible mystery to the finite understanding of the human mind:
- the best a person can do is muddle through life to the best of one's ability
- stand in awe at the mysterious projection of an abstract deity-figure.

Extremism (Knowable):

Empiricism
- to know about God: attributes, characteristics is to know God.

Ontologism - universal intuitive knowledge of God.

Mysticism - ethereal, esoteric, Gnostic knowing of God.

Union/oneness knowledge of God Diminishment of awe, reverence, worship.

God's Self-revelation

Dialectic – Both/And

Extremism	Historical	Relational	Extremism
Historicism Objectivism	Historical disclosure of Himself.	Relational personal disclosure of Himself.	Subjectivism Existentialism Personalism
Fundamentalism	Jn. 3:16 - "God so loved the world that He gave His only begotten Son..."	Gal. 1:12 - "I received it by revelation of Jesus Christ"	Mysticism Experientialism
"God in a box" "God in a book" "God in strait-jacket"	Jn. 1:1,14 - "Word was made flesh" - incarnation I Tim. 2:5 - "one mediator between God and man."	Eph. 1:13 - "revelation in the knowledge of Him" Phil. 3:15 - "God will reveal it to you."	Progressivism Relativism "Everything subject to change – no absolutes."
Proceduralism Unchangeableness of God can be used to construct fixed system of God's predetermined and prescribed action. - God's ways - *ordo salutis*	I Tim. 4:10 - "Savior of all men" Jn. 19:30 - "It is finished!" II Tim. 1:10 - "Jesus abolished death and brought life and immortality..." Historical revelation of God in Christ is singular and complete.	Personal revelation of God to individuals. "Revelation is caught, not taught" Divine relativity in His variable *modus operandi* of revealing Himself uniquely & novelly to the hearts of His people.	Process theology God changes to correspond to each personal relationship. Accomodationism

God's Grace Action

Dialectic – Both/And

YES	NO
Positive action/*via positiva* II Cor. 1:19,20	Negative action/*via negativa*
..to invite mankind into participation/fellowship with Himself.	..to victory and supremacy of Satan.
..to grace towards mankind	..to the power of sin over mankind
..to love the world via Jesus Christ (Jn. 3:16)	..to humanities being lost in the Fall
..to the cross to effect death in order to grant life	..to disordered, dysfunctional, abused, misued humanity
..to raise Jesus from dead	..to divine punishment or judgment after Fall.
..to give Jesus' resurrection life to receptive persons	..to natural law & religion
..to salvation in Christ (Acts 4:12; Rom. 1:16)	..to making the Law and human performance the way to God.
..to reconciliation of God with mankind.	..to death consequences of sin as last word.
..to restoration of humanity	**JESUS** took the **NO** on behalf of all humanity.
..to sufficiency of His grace for all Christian life.	
JESUS is the **YES** of God	

← Extremism

Arrogant Religion

.. pride of having correct knowledge and interpretation of God's YES action in Jesus Christ.

.. pride of perfectionism and triumphalism, by denyig grace of God's NO.

The YES will be continually perverted if the NO is not held simultaneously.

← Extremism

Negative Religion

..focusing on the demonic as having power over mankind.

..focusing on sin-consciousness & alleged alienation from God.

..focusing on morality and human performance for relationship with God.

The NO is for the sake of the YES, not its own sake.

GOD

Dialectic – Both/And

JUST	MERCIFUL
God manifests His character fairly and reasonably.	God is merciful to deliver us from slavery to sin.
God hates sin that is contrary to His character. - consequence - God is FOR us	Faithful to His character of Love (cf. I Jn. 4:8,16), He delivers us by Son, Jesus.
God acts fairly to make right what mankind cannot make right by himself, and make receptive persons righteous with His righteousness.	God's mercy is actively expressed in His grace - non-transactional - not performance-based Heb. 4:16 - "receive mercy & find grace in need"
Isa. 30:18 - "Lord is God of justice" Ps. 89:14 - "righteousness and justice."	Ps. 89:14,28 - "lovingkindness forever" Ps. 145:9 - "His mercies are all over His works" Isa. 30:18 - "Lord longs to be gracious to you"

Extremism

Legalism

Viewing God from law paradigm.

God projected as punitive
- severe & rigid.

Forensic justice of God.
- Will objectively declare a person "righteous" without making said person righteous.

Extremism

Sentimentalism

God's loving mercy cancels the just consequences of sin.

God's benevolent grace overlooks man's disobedience.

Universalism
- automatic, wholesale eternal salvation for all mankind.

God's Grace

Dialectic – Both/And

← Extremism

← Extremism

Ontological	Dynamic
Being of God	... in Action (doing)
Provision - Personal Presence	Function - God at Work
"Grace is a Person" - God's grace always involves His personal presence of "Being"	Phil. 2:13 – "God is at work in you to will and to work for His good pleasure."
Triune Being of God in the relationality of Father, Son, and Holy Spirit	Christological realization of God's action - Jn. 1:17 – "grace and truth realized in Jesus Christ"
Divine Being is always manifested in Triune divine action.	Dynamic of divine action cannot be separated from divine Being.
God in His Trinitarian fullness is fully invested in His every action.	God *Does* what He *Does* because He *IS* who He *IS*

Extremism (Ontological side):

Deistic transcendence separates and detaches God from the happenings of the created world
- separated concept of God in much religious thought.
- God becomes an idealistic abstraction; a "no show" in the events of human lives.

Extremism (Dynamic side):

Alleged "benefits" of God apart from the Being of God.

"Virtual Reality" of divine action

"Means of Grace"
- Eucharist
- "disciplines"

Specified actions indicative of God

Satan

Dialectic – Both/And

Extremism	**Derivative Creature**	**Originator of Evil**	Extremism
Reasoning from the supreme "sovereignty" of God and the derivativeness of Satan, some conclude:	Lucifer, the Light-bearer, was designed to derive from the "God who is light, and in Whom there is no darkness at all" (I Jn. 1:5).	Lucifer, by his choice to oppose God as adversary, became Satan, the devil. Still deriving from God, not an "independent self," Satan distorts and reverses the good character of God, thus originating and becoming the source of the character of evil.	Dualism views Satan as Evil One equal in power to the goodness of God.
- God is the source of evil character. cf. Isa. 45:7 (KJB); James 1:13	As a choosing derivative creature he inexplicably chose to defy God with the dark character of selfishness. - Isa. 14:14 - "I will make myself like the Most High"	Acts 13:10 (to Elymas) "you son of the devil, ... you make crooked the straight ways of God"	- regarded as a stalemate wherein neither can overcome the other.
"Satan is just the backside of God" "Satan is just God's errand boy" "Satan is just the left hand of God"	Despite Satan's selfish choice to make himself the Evil One and the source of all selfishness, contrary to God's love, he is still derivative creature.	II Cor. 4:4 - "god of this world" I Jn. 2:13,14; 3:12; 5:18 - "the Evil One" Eph. 5:8; 6:12; Col. 1:13; I Pt. 2:9 - "darkness"	Some emphases on spiritual warfare and deliverance elevate Satan's power of evil, failing to understand the victory of Jesus.

Satan

Dialectic – Both/And

← Extremism

← Extremism

Necessary	Freely Self-chosen	Extremism
Satan is the necessary negative to God's Positive	Lucifer, the light-bearer, was a derivative angelic creature with freedom of choice.	Theodicy – the attempt to explain how evil entered God's righteous world.
For human beings to have genuine freedom of choice it was necessary that a genuine spiritual alternative be available.	Lucifer freely chose to defy and challenge God. Isa. 14:14 – "I will be like the Most High God"	Ultimate incongruity of how derivative creature could choose a character other than God when there was no known spiritual source for such.
This must not be construed to imply that God in His absolute goodness and righteousness is the author or source of evil or sin.	In so doing, Lucifer became Satan, the adversary, the Evil opposite of God, the "ruler of this world" (Jn. 12:31; 16:11), the "god of this age" (II Cor. 4:4), and the source of all self-oriented character and sinfulness.	

← Extremism

Logical negativism must not be allowed to lead to the conclusion of a dualistic standoff or stalemate between two equal forces or powers.

Neither is Satan to be regarded as merely the absence or privation of God and His character.

Satan

Dialectic – Both/And

Extremism	Limitation	Extensivity	Extremism
Satan is defeated by Jesus Christ and totally impotent.	Satan (spirit-being) is not a god (divine-being), despite references to the - "god of this age" I Cor 4:4 - "ruler of this world" (Jn. 12:31; 14:30; 16:11)	Satan (spirit-being) does not have the same limitations that mankind (human-beings) have. - humans are contextualized by space and time: - localized in space - temporalized in time	Devil regarded as so pervasive in fallen world - suspicious paranoia
devil is bound, chained, and locked up - cannot harm Christians in any manner.	Satan is not: - omnipotent - limitation of power. - omniscient - limitation of knowledge - omnipresent - limitation of presence; not infinite God - omnilocative Man - unilocative Satan - translocative	As spirit-being, Satan is not temporalized in time. - tempted Adam, Job, Jesus, us, across centuries. Satan not localized in space - tempts persons around the world simultaneously	"Satan is the back-side of God" "Satan is God's errand boy"
"Jesus put Satan in a strait-jacket" Satan is a toothless charlatan, and not a threat to anyone.	Limitation of Satan by the redemptive work of Christ (Matt. 12:29; Rev. 20:2)	"prince of the power of the air" (Eph. 2:2)	There are those who are suspiciously looking for the "devil/demons behind every bush"

Humanity

Dialectic – Both/And

Extremism ←	Derivative Being	Determinative Being	Extremism →
Determinism - either diabolic or divine determinism. Human beings regarded as automatons.	Extrinsic being - derived outside of oneself.	God's Self-limitation of Himself avoids absolute determinism, and provides for freely-chosen faith-love personal relationship between God and humans.	Human Autonomy
Augustinian-Calvinism is the primary system that denies self-determinative responsibility toward God, indicating that God has predetermined the choices and actions of human persons by predestination.	Derived origin & function - do not exist *a se*, in themselves - do not function *ek autos* out of themselves.	With "freedom of choice" humans are free to choose the derivational source of their spiritual, psychological and physiological function.	Humanistic premise of persons as independent, autonomous beings, capable of self-generating their own character and activity. - Independent selves.
	Human function is dependent upon a spirit-source, either God or Satan (*ek Theos* or *ek diabolos*). From spirit-source humans derive character, identity, image and destiny by the receptivity of faith.	Humans have responseability by which to respond to God's action to redeem/ restore humanity in the Person/work of Jesus: - Personal rejection - Person reception	Premise of human sovereignty.
	No human individual is an "independent self."		Theological form called Pelagianism or Arminianism.

Humanity

Dialectic – Both/And

Extremism →

Extremism →

Created in God's Image	Solidarity with Sin
Gen. 1:27 - "God created man in His own image, in the image of God He created him" - does not imply there is something about man that is like God - indicates that man created for visible expression of character of God. In the Fall of man into sin, man lost image of God. Restored to God's image by the presence and function of the divine Christ in the spirit of an individual. Col. 3:10 - "put on the new self who is being renewed to a true knowledge according to the image of the One who created him"	Rom. 5:19 - "through the one man's (*Adam's*) disobedience the many were made sinners" Rom. 3:23 - "all have sinned and come short of the glory of God" Solidarity with sin does not imply man has essential, inherent character of sin. Man is not a devil! - it does imply an association, identity with the Satanic source of sin. -being "made sinners" indicates a spiritual identity whereby the "prince of the power of the air becomes the spirit that works in the sons of disobedience" (Eph. 2:2,3)

Extremism

Humanism
- undue elevation of humanity

God created "little gods" capable of independent and self-generative function.
- by free-will man determines his own character.
- by good choices man resembles, represents or reflects divine image/character.

Extremism

Augustinianism
- undue devaluation of humanity

Total depravity.
- totality of human being and function is degraded
- incapable of functioning as a human creature who can respond to God.
- vile, deficient, debased humanity
- "just an animal"

Human Personhood

Dialectic – Both/And

I — Individuality	**We** — Relationality
Greek *ego* - word for "I" Freud used differently.	Human relationality based on Trinitarian relationality
Individual choosing – creatures with freedom of choice (not "free-will"). Mind, emotion, will	Personhood is relational "I-Thou" relationships - not psychological "personhood"
Dependent, derivative creatures response-able to derive from spirit-source.	Social creatures "no man is an island" "in this together" Regard for what is greater than ourselves
The human collective is only as good as the character of the individuals within the collective.	Greek *koinonia*- fellowship, commonality, participation Church - *ecclesia* "called out" to function together. Interactive Body of Christ.

Extremism (I)

Individualism
Autonomy
Independent Self

"Every man for himself."
"Go it alone"
"Do your own thing"
"Be all you can be"
Narcissism

Self-made man
Self-centered
Self-serving

Greek *idiotes* - those who refused when "called out" for town meeting (*ecclesia*)

Extremism (We)

Socialism
Associationism
- identity, meaning purpose only in the whole.

Communism
Ecclesiasticism
Hierarchialism
Institutionalism

"Group-think"
party-mentality
peer pressure
herd-behavior
political-correctness.

"Don't settle for a collective that will not allow you to be yourself."

Human Response

Dialectic – Both/And

Extremism	Belief	Faith	Extremism
Epistemological belief systems	Assent, consent to facts Acts 16:30 - "believe on the Lord Jesus Christ."	Receptivity, availability, abandonment to God Jn. 1:12- "as many received"	Passivism
Creedalism	Belief - creedal statements - coherence, concensus of thought - figured out - accomplishes certitude	Gal. 3:1 - "received by hearing with faith." Gal. 2:6 - "as received (by faith), so walk in Him"	Challenge fo all belief-systems - "don't tell me what to believe"
Fundamentalism - willing to fight and die for what is considered a correct order of beliefs. - self-justification	Belief is foundational! Belief is static! - rigid, inflexible, dead Belief seeks answers - wallows in words - seeks definitive content	Faith is functional! Faith is dynamic! - in motion, alive Faith questions everything - listens to God - seeks personal revelation	Individualism Separatism - non-conformity
Religionism Religion is built on rigidity and inflexibility of beliefs.	Belief is informational Belief cannot tolerate doubt and uncertainty. Belief provides the building-blocks for religion.	Faith is incarnational Faith finds its springboard in questioning and doubt. Faith is the dead-end for all religion.	Anti-authority - anarchism
Importance of apologetics	Belief responds to doctrine and reasoned teaching Belief is obstacle to faith.	Faith responds to the grace activity of the Triune God Faith seeks relationality.	Repudiation of apologetics and systematic theology.

Human Relational Function

Dialectic – Both/And

← Extremism | | | Extremism →

Spiritual Determinism	Spiritual Relationality	Psychological Relationionity	Humanistic Behavioral Determinism
- Divine determinism.	Spirit-based relationality that allows spirit-character to pervade human relational interactions.	Relationality based on human personality and individuality	
- Diabolic determinism			Humanism denies spiritual relationality.
Denial of human capability to participate in relational function.	Personhood based on interpersonal relations	Personhood based on psychological function	- posits that man is "independent self" capable of self-generating own character.
- Augustinian premise of "total depravity"	- Cannot be a person in a vacuum without relationality.	- function of mind, emotion and will of individual is basis of personality	- peronhood is intrinsic to one's own being.
- Perfectionistic premise of "entire sanctification"…	- Human beings designed by Triune God to participate in Trinitarian relationality of perfect love, community, fellowship…	- temperament patterns display differently. (Hippocrates - choleric, sanquine, phlegmatic, melancholy)	
Spiritualism	Adamic Fall of mankind into sin, allowed for diabolic relationality.	Patterned desires of "Flesh"	Psychologism
	- selfish and destructive sociological conflict.	- Individuated patterns of selfishness and sinfulness in human desires, such as prejudices, biases, etc.	Behavioralism

©2014 by James A. Fowler

Jesus Christ

Dialectic – Both/And

GOD	MAN
Deity, divinity, Son of God	Humanity, Son of Man, Individual human being
Jn. 1:1 - "and the Word was God"	Acts 2:22 - "a man attested to you by God"
Jn. 5:18 - "making Himself equal with God"	Rom. 5:15 - "the One Man, Jesus Christ"
Phil. 2:6 - "He existed in the form of God"	I Cor. 15:21 - "by a man came resurrection"
Col. 2:9 - "In Him the fullness of deity dwells"	Phil. 2:8 - "found in appearance as a man"
Titus 2:13 - "God and Savior Christ Jesus"	I Tim. 2:5 - "the man, Christ Jesus

Extremism (MAN)

Ebionites
Jesus just a man elected to be and act as Son of God.

Adoptionism
Jesus a man adopted by God and given Christ-cloak or Messiah-mantle

Arianism
Denied deity of Jesus, accepting form of Adoptionism.

Radical kenoticism. Jesus "emptied Himself of divinity."

Hypostatic Union

The council of Chalcedon in AD 451 explained that the "two natures" (divine and human) were united into one personal individual, the God-man, Jesus Christ.

Jn. 1:14 - "the Word was made flesh"
Heb. 2:14 - "He Himself partook of flesh and blood"
This has been orthodox Christian teaching ever since.

Extremism (GOD)

Docetism
Greek *dokein* "to appear." Jesus only appeared to be human, a "phantom."

Apolllinarianism
Divine *logos* replaced human spirit and soul, so Jesus only had human body as container-vessel.

Absorptionism
Jesus' humanity was absorbed or subsumed into His divine Being.

Jesus Christ

Dialectic – Both/And

	Humiliation	Exaltation	
Extremism ↓			↑ **Extremism**

Extremism (Humiliation side)	Humiliation	Exaltation	Extremism (Exaltation side)
Negativism Inordinate emphasis on humiliation of Jesus can lead to macabre expressions. - *The Passion* Evangelicalism has often emphasized death on cross over resurrection Failure to see *Christus Victor* motif. Undue emphasis on wretchedness, sin-consciousness.	Lowliness, debasement Isa. 53 - "despised, forsaken, acquainted with grief" • Birth Phil 2:7 - "emptied Himself, likeness of man" Gal. 4:4 - "born of woman (in stable) under the Law" • Temptation Heb. 4:15 - "tempted in all points as we are" • Washing disciples' feet Cf. • Suffering, pathos I Pet. 4:1 - "Christ suffered in the flesh" • Crucifixion Phil 2:8 - "humbled Himself .. to point of death" • Burial - bowels of earth I Cor. 15:4 - "...buried"	Lifted up, elevated Heb. 7:26 - "exalted above the heavens." • Resurrection Acts 10:40 "God raised Him up on third day." Rom. 1:4 - "declared Son of God with power by the resurrection from death" • Ascension Acts 2:34 - "ascended" • Glorification Jn. 13:31 - "Now is the Son of Man glorified. • Coronation Heb. 12:2 - "sat down at right hand of throne of God." • Intercession Heb. 7:25 - "He always lives to make intercession"	Positivism Triumphalism Ecstaticism Failure to recognize that exaltation comes via humiliation. - the same is true still as Christ works in the life of the Christian.

Jesus Christ

Dialectic – Both/And

← Extremism	Prototype	Provision	Extremism →
Imitationism Mimicry Performance	Model of the Christ-life. Exemplary	Modality of Christian life. Jn. 14:6 - "I am the way."	Passivism Acquiesence Quietism
"monkey see, monkey do."	Jn. 13:15 - "I gave you an example that you should do as I did"	Jn. 15:5 - "Apart from Me, you can do nothing."	"It's not what we do, but what Christ does."
Are we to "parrot" or "ape" Jesus?	Phil. 4:5 - "have this attitude which was in Christ Jesus" I Cor. 11:1 - "be imitators, as I am of Christ."	Gal. 2:20 - "It is no longer I who lives, but Christ lives in me."	The greatest sin of Christians today is to try to live the Christian life."
Imitation of Christ Thomas A Kempis	Heb. 12:2 - "keep your eyes on Jesus, pioneer and perfector of faith"	Phil. 4: "I can do all things through Christ who strengthens me." I Thess. 5:24 - "He will bring it to pass."	
In His Steps Charles Sheldon	I Pet. 2:21 - "Christ left you an example for you to follow in His steps."	Christ lives "as" us – we are the only epistles of Christ that some will ever see.	"Just go with the flow of the Jesus-life."
WWJD - "What Would Jesus Do?"	Jesus lived out the Christ-life perfectly for every moment in time for 33 years.	Jesus wants to live that same life in you/me; to re-present Himself to the world in which we live.	"Let go, and let God"

©2014 by James A. Fowler

Jesus Christ

Dialectic – Both/And

Extremism	Savior	Lord	Extremism
Easy-believism	To make another "safe"	Authority over another	Lordship Salvation
Revivalism - get people "down the aisle to get saved"	Matt. 1:21 - "call His name Jesus, for He will save His People from their sins"	Matt. 28:18 - "All authority is given to Me in heaven and on earth"	Ethical behaviorism
Mental assent to Jesus as deliverer - "off the hook" - "spiritual fire insurance policy" - salvation as "pass into heaven"	Matt. 18:4 - "Son of Man has come to save what is lost" Jn. 4:42 - "this One is indeed the Savior of the world" Rom. 1:16 - "gospel is the power of God for salvation"	Rom. 10:9 - "If you confess with you mouth Jesus as Lord, you will be saved" Acts 2:36 - "God has made Him both Lord and Christ" Phil. 2:11 - "every tongue will confess that Jesus Christ is Lord" II Pet. 3:18 - "grow in the grace and knowledge of our Lord and Savior, Jesus Christ"	Pietism that tends to demand expression of character-fruit in order to qualify as "Christian." - become "fruit inspectors"
Emphasize "faith alone" without "works"	I Tim. 2:4 - "desires all men to be saved" Titus 1:4 - "Christ Jesus our Savior"	Proper response to Jesus includes repentance.	Tendency to demand performance assurance of "total commitment" & obedience
Views "Jesus is Lord" as assent to deity ... God	I Jn. 4:14 - "The Father has sent the Son to be the Savior of the world"		

Jesus Christ

Dialectic – Both/And

Physical Christ	Pneumatic Christ

Extremism

Jesus viewed primarily as Spirit-being who mystically relates to the spirit...
- of all mankind?
- of those human beings receptive to Him by faith.

Some indicate it is inconsequential whether Jesus ever lived as an historical person.

Where is Jesus?
- "Father's right hand"

Reabsorbed into God?

Pneumatic Christ

Spiritual Jesus
Experiential Jesus

I Cor. 15:45 - "the Last Adam became the life-giving Spirit.

Rom. 1:4 - "Spirit of holiness, Jesus our Lord"

II Cor. 3:17 - "Lord is the Spirit"

I Cor. 6:17 - "joined to the Lord, one spirit with Him

Rom. 8:9 - "if do not have the Spirit of Christ, none of His"

Rom. 8:11 - "His Spirit dwells in you"

Gal. 4:6 - "God sent tSpirit of His Son into our hearts."

Phil. 1:19 - "the provision of the Spirit of Christ."

Physical Christ

Historical Jesus
Incarnated Jesus

Jn. 1:14 - the Word became flesh"

Rom. 8:3 - "God sent His Son in the likeness of sinful flesh..."

I Tim. 3:16 - "He was revealed in the flesh, and vindicated in the Spirit"

Heb. 2:14 - "He Himself partook of flesh and blood

I John 1:1 - "we have seen with our eyes, touched with our hands, the Word of life."

Extremism

Jesus viewed only or primarily as physical personage of history almost two millennia ago.

Academic research seeking the "real historical Jesus."

Historical society for the remembrance of Jesus.

Where is Jesus?
- "dead and gone!"

Is He the eternal God-man?

81

Sin

Dialectic – Both/And

Human actions	Spiritual character	
Common tendency among religious persons to identify "sin" by particular human acts and behaviors	Broadly and generally defined, sin is any/all character contrary to the character of God's perfection and righteousness.	Some will reason: - "If an individual derives all character and is not the generative source of sin or righteousness, then our responsibility is simply to "let go and let God" be and do what He wants to be and do in our lives."
Human actions are only sinful when pervaded and energized by the character of the Evil One.	Such antithetical character is energized by the Evil One, Satan, the originator of all evil character.	
No external action of a human individual is to be regarded as intrinsically sin or sinful. Jn. 3:19; 7:7 - "deeds are evil" Gal. 5:19 - "deeds of the flesh" Jude 15 - "ungodly deeds" I Tim. 5:24 - "sins quite evident"	Human beings are incapable of self-generating evil character in sinful actions - I Jn. 3:8 - "one who practices sin is of the devil"	
	When a human individual derives evil character" in their behavioral actions they commit "sins."	Passivism Acquiesence

Religion has keyed in on the externalities of various behavioral actions, admonishing people to: "Do this; Don't do that!" "Thou shalt; Thou shalt not!"

This moralizing focus on human behavioralism inevitably leads to legalistic attempts to regulate behavior.

Sin

Dialectic – Both/And

→ Extremism

→ Extremism

Diabolic	Human Responsibility
Satan is the *prima causa peccati*, primary source of evil and sinful character in the world and in human behavior.	Human freedom of choice makes us responsible for the choice of being receptive to sinful character that is contrary to and misrepresentative of the character of Christ.
I Jn. 3:8 - "one doing sin is of (*ek* - derives "out of") the devil" Matt.16:23 - "Get thee behind Me, Satan" John 8:34 - "everyone who commits sin is slave of sin" Rom. 5:21 - "sin reigned in death" Rom. 6:17 - "you were slaves of sin"	Human choice to allow for sinful expression is the *causa secunda* (secondary cause) of sin in human behavior. It is the means by which we connect with the Satanic source of evil and sinful character.
Sin is not equivalent to Satan, but is the character Satan originates.	Rom. 6:14 - "sin shall not be master over you" Rom. 14:23 - "whatever is not of faith is sin"

Left extremism (Diabolic):

Diabolic Determinism - failure to take into account human responsibility of choice has led some to determinism.

Flip Wilson comedy routine: "The Devil made me do it!"

Contemporary culture has advocated removing the onus of any fault or responsibility of sin.

Right extremism (Human Responsibility):

Humanism - failure to recognize the Satanic source of sin, necessarily leads to the conclusion that a human being is an "independent self" who is capable of self-generating the character of sinfulness and selfishness.

Evangelicalism has promulgated this humanistic idea of sin.

Sin

Dialectic – Both/And

← Extremism | Extremism →

Transgression

Sin must necessarily be considered in contrast to the perfect character of God, and as a violation of the intended expression in human behavior.

Rom. 5:15-20 - "transgression/sin increased"
Eph. 2:5; Col. 2:13 - "dead in our transgressions"
Eph. 2:2 - "dead in your trespasses and sins"
Eph. 1:7 - "forgiveness of our trespasses"
Matt. 7:23 - "you who practice lawlessness."
I Jn. 3:4 - "one who practices sin practices lawlessness"

When sin is viewed only or primarily as transgression, trespass or lawlessness, it is being considered as an objective act outside of oneself.

This can result in a detached and legalistic perspective of sin.

Independence

Man is not an "independent self," capable of manufacturing or producing any form of character - godly or sinful.

When duped by the diabolic deceiver the human individual can falsely believe in his/her alleged "independence."

The lie of the serpent offered such sinful independence - "you, too, can be like God" (Gen. 3:5), -
- independent
- autonomous
- self-generative

Humanism is the fallacious lie of human independence and self-potential.

Evangelical humanism is rampant in American religion, advocating that the human being is the source of his/her own sinfulness.

Atonement

Dialectic – Both/And

← Extremism

→ Extremism

Analogic

Christian redemptive thought has often been based on analogies of the atoning action of Jesus Christ:

Liberation concept
Legal/Penal concept
Purification concept
Necrological concept
Sacrificial concept
Covenantal concept
Economic concept
Transactional concept
Triumphal concept
Vital concept
Spiritual concept
Functional concept
Relational concept
Ontological concept

Throughout the history of Christian thought various redemption and atonement theories have served as the springboards for theological systems that emphasize a particular facet of biblical truth, but fail to explain the fullness of Christ's Person and work.

Christocentric

The work of God in Christ is best explained by the Person of Jesus Christ, rather than by using illustrative analogies.

Analogies tend to direct attention to the "benefits" of Christ's work, whereas Christocentric explanation focuses on the beneficence of the Being of Jesus Christ.

All of His benefit is in His Being!

All that He did and does is indicative and expressive of His Being. His every act is invested and energized by His very Being.

Evangelical Calvinism
- emphasizes the Being of Christ as deity and humanity were united in the hypostatic union of the Person of Jesus.
- Vicarious humanity of Jesus
- Incarnational Atonement

Salvation

Dialectic – Both/And

	ALL	NOT ALL	
Extremism			**Extremism**

Extremism (left): Universalism

General

ALL humanity destined to spend eternity in heaven. This is not predicated on any human response.

Determinist

ALL humanity deterministically subsumed into incarnational life and ministry of Jesus. His vicarious humanity incorporates all human beings into Him for eternity.

ALL

Objective Universal - "Finished work" of Jesus makes salvation available to ALL mankind.

ALL loved - Jn. 3:16
ALL redeemed - Eph. 1:7
ALL forgiven - Jn. 1:29
All made righteous - Rom. 5:18,19
ALL reconciled - Rom. 5:10,11
ALL given life - Rom. 5:18
ALL saved - Titus 2:11
ALL blessed - Eph. 1:3
ALL drawn to Christ - Jn. 12:32

Objective realities are valid whether an individual believes it or not.

NOT ALL

Subjective Particular - Not ALL receive living Lord Jesus. Some reject God's Grace.

Human beings are choosing creatures with "freedom of choice." This choice has no merit!

Faith is not a "work" nor a "gift of God" but is our receptivity of God's activity.

Either-or particularization: Some receive; some reject

Reception of divine indwelling presence of Triune God.

Extremism (right): Particularism

Objective

ALL qualified to mean "all of God's predestined "elect." Salvation denied to "non-elect."

Subjective

ALL qualified to apply only to those who respond in faith according to particular religious procedures.

Salvation

Dialectic – Both/And

Extremism →

→ Objective

Subjective ←

← Extremism

Objective

The Person and work of Jesus Christ is objectively efficacious for the salvation of all mankind.

Everything necessary for the salvation of mankind was accomplished.

All of humanity is "made safe" and delivered from the consequences of sin by the death of Jesus.

I Tim. 4:10 - "living God is Savior of all men, especially believers"

Titus 2:11 - "the grace of God has appeared bringing salvation to all men"

Jn. 3:17 - "God sent His Son into the world, that the world might be saved through Him."

Subjective

Subjective acceptance and receptivity of Christ particularizes an individual's experience of salvation.

Individual is "made safe" from death to live by the indwelling Jesus.

Acts 16:30,31 - "Believe in the Lord Jesus Christ, and you will be saved."

Eph. 2:8,9 - "For by grace you have been saved through faith."

Rom. 10:8-10 - "confess with mouth, believe in heart, you will be saved."

I Cor. 1:21 - "God was well-pleased to save those who believe"

Rom. 5:10 - "saved by His life"

Extremism

Evangelical Calvinism emphasizes the *fait accompli* of objective salvation in the incarnation and crucifixion of the historical Jesus, while essentially denying that an individual can or should respond in faith to the gospel of Jesus Christ

Extremism

Evangelicals often view salvation as a static personal event of conversion wherein an individual "gets saved" by the personal choice to receive Jesus.

In so doing they ever so subtely imply that the individual contributes to their own salvation by their faith-action.

Salvation

Dialectic – Both/And

Augustinianism Calvinism

-ontological re-ductionism of fallen humanity, whereby humans are deemed defective and incapable of responding to God's divine initiative of grace.

- grace is misconstrued as divine determinism whereby God sovereignly" elects some for salvation and others to perdition.

Grace

Divine initiative

Eph. 2:5,8 - "for by grace you have been saved..."

Grace is the divine dynamic of God's action via the Son Jesus Christ (cf. Jn 1:17), and by the Spirit.

Acts 15:11 - "saved through the grace of Lord Jesus"
Titus 2:11 - "the grace of God has appeared bringing salvation to all men."
II Tim. 1:9 - "saved us according to His own purpose and grace.."
I Pet. 1:10 - "this salvation, the prophets prophesied of the grace to come{

Faith

Human response

Eph. 2:8 - "...saved through faith"

Faith is the human choice of receptivity of the activity of the Triune God, both initially and continually in the Christian life.

Acts 16:31 - "believe in the Lord Jesus... be saved"
II Tim. 3:15 - "salvation through faith in Christ"
II Thess. 2:13 - "chosen for salvation...through faith in the truth"
I Pt. 1:9 - "outcome of your faith, the salvation of your souls"

Pelagianism
- a human being's volitional choice determines and effects his/her participation in salvation.

Arminianism
- not as radically humanistic, but does emphasize human faith-choice for human obedience and performance.

Evangelicalism
- tends to focus on human action and performance

Salvation

Dialectic – Both/And

← Extremism	Faith	Works	Extremism →
Fideism Protestant repudiation of "good works" for justification spilled over to minimizing "good works" in Christian behavior. "faith without works is dead, non-existent, impotent, vacuous, and does not qualify as faith."	Human faith, receptivity of Christ's redemptive activity, cannot be supplemented by human activity or "works." Rom. 3:28 - "justified by faith apart from works of the law." Christian faith, receptivity of Christ's activity in the Christian life, is rendered meaningless and void if active outworking is not evident. James 2:17 - "faith, if it has no works, is dead, being by itself." James 2:20 - "faith without works is vacuous"	Human "works" and performance have no meritorious benefit towards personal salvation. Eph. 2:8,9 - "by grace you have been saved through faith, ...not of works lest anyone should boast." Claim of Christian faith without the outworking of Christ's character and ministry is invalid. James 2:20 - "faith without works is useless" James 2:24 - "man is justified by works, and not by faith alone." James 2:26 - "faith without works is dead"	Human performance Roman Catholic theology has tended toward humanistic potentialism and human contribution to God's favor. "show me your works, and I'll show you that it could only be derived from the character of God.

Salvation

Dialectic – Both/And

Extremism → Security	Apostasy ← Extremism
Latin word *securus*, "without care of anxiety"	Greek word *apostasia* - "to stand away from Jesus by renouncing Him"
Heb. 5:9 - "to all that obey Him, the source of eternal salvation"	I Tim. 4:1 - "some will fall away from the faith"
I John 5:13 - "you may know that you have eternal life"	Heb. 3:12 - "falling away from the living God"
I Cor. 1:8 - "Jesus Christ shall confirm you to the end"	Heb. 6:4-6 - "tasted of heavenly gift and then fallen away"
Phil. 1:6 - "He will perfect it until the day of Jesus Christ."	John 15:6 - "If anyone does not abide in Me, he is thrown away.."
Heb. 12:2 - "Jesus, the pioneer and perfecter of our faith"	I Cor. 9:27 - "lest I should be disqualified"
I Pet. 1:5 - "protected by the power of God."	Gal. 5:4 - "you have been severed from Christ... fallen from grace"

Extremism (Security side):

"Eternal security" is a doctrine originating in the Augustinian/ Calvinistic theological tradition.

Baptistic explanation of "once saved, always saved."

Must differentiate between static and dynamic security.
- Divine preservation and human perseverance.

Extremism (Apostasy side):

Apostasy is a doctrine emphasized more by Arminians who place more emphasis on human choice.

"Once apostasized always apostasized" (Heb. 6:6)

Calvinists deny that such persons were ever identified with Jesus and participating in salvation.

Regeneration

Dialectic – Both/And

	Conversion	Union	
Extremism			**Extremism**

Extremism

There is an "easy-believism rampant in the Western churches that reduces becoming a Christian to merely:
- assent to facts
- raising hands
- walking an aisle
- confessing one's mistakes
- changing one's mind-set
- repeating a creed
- getting baptized
- joining a church
- promising to keep the rules

Conversion

The conversion of regeneration involves the radical exchange from a condition of spiritual death to spiritual life.

Matt. 18:3 - "unless converted, you will not enter kingdom of heaven"

Jn. 3:3,7 - "must be born again...to see kingdom."

I Pt. 1:3 - "born again to a living hope."

Acts 26:18 - " to turn/convert them from darkness to light, from dominion of Satan to God...receive forgiveness of sins"

Titus 3:5 - "saved us by the washing of regeneration"

Union

Eastern Orthodox concept of *Theosis*, requires indwelling presence of living Christ and energizing function of living Lord Jesus. Christians do not become the "essence" of Jesus, but do participate in the "energies" (functional empowering) of the living Christ.

II Pt. 1:4 - "partakers of the divine nature"

I Cor. 6:17 - "he who is joined to the Lord is one spirit with Him."

Heb. 3:14 - "partakers of Christ"

Heb. 6:4 - "partakers of the Holy Spirit"

Extremism

Overly objectified concepts of "union with Christ" view union as an historical event or juridical declaration/transaction

Some subjective emphases on "union life" have veered into:
- pantheism
- panentheism
- monistic merging/mingling of Christian and Christ.

Mysticism

Adoption

Dialectic – Both/And

043

©2014 by James A. Fowler

Objective

God the Father, through the divine-human Son, has eliminated all estrangement with fallen humanity and accomplished everything necessary to adopt the entire human race as sons and daughters into one big family of God.

Gal. 4:4-7 - "God sent forth His Son...that we might receive adoption as sons... no longer a slave, but a son."

Eph. 1:4-8 - "predestined to adoption as sons through Jesus Christ"

Subjective

The relational experience of functioning as an adopted child of God in fellowship with the Triune God is predicated on a personal response of faith receptivity to divine presence and activity.

Gal. 4:6 - "you are sons, God has sent forth the Spirit of His Son into our hearts"

Rom. 8:15 - "you have received a spirit of adoption as sons"

Gal. 3:7,26 - "sons of God through faith in Christ Jesus"

Extremism →

Universalism - all humanity is adopted by God into the eternal and heavenly family of Christ

Denial of humanity's capability or response-ability to make personal response to God's action in Jesus Christ.

Evangelical Calvinism

Extremism →

Individualism - some maintain that the human act of faith contributes to or effects an individual's salvation.

Pelagianism
Arminianism
Evangelicalism

92

Sanctification

Dialectic – Both/And

Initial	Continual
Extremism ←	→ Extremism
Accomplished, complete, entire sanctification	Progressively expressed holy character
Objectively made available by Christ; subjectively realized in regeneration.	Greek *hagiasmos* - the process by which the Holy character of the Triune God is allowed to be expressed in Christian behavior.
Eph. 5:26 - "He gave Himself to sanctify her"	II Cor. 7:1 - "perfecting holiness in fear of God"
Heb. 10:10 - "sanctified through the offering of Jesus Christ once for all"	I Thess. 4:3 - "will of God, your sanctification"
I Cor. 1:2 - "those who are sanctified, saints ..."	I Thess. 5:23 - "may God of peace sanctify you entirely in spirit, soul, body"
I Cor. 1:30 - "Jesus became to us sanctification"	Heb. 12:10 - "that we may share His holiness"
I Cor. 6:11 - "you were sanctified in the name of the Lord Jesus Christ"	Heb. 12:14 - "pursue holiness ... to see the Lord"
Heb. 2:11 - "those sanctified are all of one Father"	

Initial — Extremism:

Perfectionism

Holiness movement: (Wesley) - emphasized "entire sanctification" in a "second blessing" that imputes Christian with sinless perfection and holiness.

Christians have spiritual identity of being "saints" - holy ones, but are not essentially holy as God is.

Continual — Extremism:

Legalism
Pietism
Moralism
Experientialism
Behavioralism
Suppressionism
Crucifixionism

Subjective personal holiness has often been pursued by religious self-effort. It can only be experienced by the dynamic grace of God in Jesus Christ.

Righteousness

Dialectic – Both/And

Extremism ↑

Objective	Subjective
Jesus Christ is the "Righteous One" (Acts 3:14; 7:52; 22:14; I Jn. 2:1)	Righteousness is divine, and when applied to human beings it is always derived from God.
Jesus' voluntary and vicarious death on the cross was the "righteous act" whereby the "Righteous One" endured death on our behalf, and made righteousness of life available to humanity.	The "Righteous One", Jesus Christ indwells the Christian, and desires to live out His Righteous character in Christian lives.
Rom. 5:18 - "through one transgression there resulted condemnation to all men, even so through one act of righteousness there resulted justification (righteousness) of life to all men."	I Cor. 1:30 - "Jesus became to us righteousness"
	Rom. 8:10 - "the spirit is alive because of righteousness"
	Rom. 5:19 - "many will be made righteous."
	II Cor. 5:19 - "we might become the righteousness of God in Him."

Extremism ↑ (Subjective side):
Humanistic religion seeks to credit an individual for performance actions (faith? good works?) alleged to be righteous or to merit a righteousness from/before God.

Mystical religion moves from derived righteousness to essential righteousness of the believer.

Extremism ↓ (Objective side):
Much of Protestantism has over-objectified the "righteous act" of Jesus Christ by emphasizing that "justification" is only the divine declaration and legal imputation of righteousness to the predetermined "elect."

Bible

Dialectic – Both/And

Extremism	**Divine Action**	**Human Action**	Extremism
Bible is the "Word of God." ...answer for every question of man. ...all God wants man to know. Christianity is the Book-religion. Bible equated with Jesus. - infallibility - deification - bibliolatry Verbal plenary inspiration. - dictation theory Authority of God vested in Bible. Literal interpretation of every word in the Bible	Divine revelation God revealed Himself naturally & supernaturally by the Son. The Bible is the record of God's revelation; not the revelation itself. Divine inspiration - God breathed - I Tim. 3:16 Divine providential preservation of textual record. Divine interpretation of Bible text by Holy Spirit. - illumination, enlightenment, personal revelation (cf. Eph. 1:17; Phil. 3:15) Bible is "word of God" in secondary sense. Jesus is "Word of God" - Jn. 1:1,14	Human historical context of Biblical documents. *sitz em leben* (setting in life). Human authors - varying vocabulary, grammar, cultural, personal perspectives Human literary constructs: historical, epistolary, apocalyptic literary styles Human collection and canonization of texts. Human interpretation : - hermeneutics Biblical criticism - critical thinking about meaning of the text Textual criticism of manuscript eviences & variance. No original mss.	Bible is just man-made book. Bible full of error and superstition Bible inspired in same sense as Shakespeare. Canonization was human process. Bible needs to be scrutinized and sanitized by demytholigization. - Form criticism - Source criticism - Redaction crit. ex. Jesus Seminar

©2014 by James A. Fowler

Kingdom

Dialectic – Both/And

	Realm	Reign	
← Extremism	When the kingdom of God is regarded as having static tangibility in a people-collective, an institution, a jurisdiction, or geographical location, it is regarded as a realm.	The kingdom of God is the dynamic reign of the Personal Lord and King, Jesus Christ in Christians' lives both individually and collectively wherever they might be.	Extremism ↑

Realm

Tangibility of Place

Lk. 4:5 - "kingdoms of the world"

Mk. 13:8 - "kingdom against kingdom"

Lk. 11:18 - "Satan ... how will his kingdom stand?"

Rev. 1:6 - "He has made us a kingdom" (cf. 5:10)

Haggai 2:2 - "I will destroy the power of the kingdoms of the nations"

Rev. 17:17 - "giving their kingdom to the Beast"

Reign

Relationality of Person

Jn. 18:36 - "My kingdom is not of this world."

I Cor. 15:50 - "flesh and blood cannot inherit the kingdom"

Rom. 14:17 - "the kingdom of God is righteousness, peace and joy"

Lk. 17:21 - "the kingdom of God is in your midst"

Col. 1:13 - "transferred us to the kingdom of His beloved Son"

Extremism (Realm)

Ecclesiasticism - some equate the visible church with the kingdom of God

Millennialism - some eschatological interpretations defer the kingdom to the future millennial period & location

Denominationalism - there are denominations who have claimed to be "the kingdom of God on earth"

Extremism (Reign)

Abstractionism
Dynamism
Etherealism
Personalism

When some Christians recognize that they are participating in the kingdom reign of the risen Lord Jesus, they sometimes become "so heavenly minded as to be of no earthly good."

Church

Dialectic – Both/And

Extremism	Organization	Organism	Extremism
Failure to understand the church as a spiritual organism has often led to a "business model" organization of church with the pastor serving as the C.E.O. When the church is just another business without divine presence and empowering, it becomes but a social irrelevancy	The church is a divine institution; divinely instituted by God. Matt. 16:18 - "Upon this rock I will build My church" A divine institution does not preclude the need for human organizational structure to implement practical functionality. - ex. national government Organizational polity may have diverse forms: - hierarchical, papal - plurality of elders, presbyterian, episcopal - congregational democracy, popular vote	The church is unique from all other social institutions. Identified as the "Body of Christ," the church is a living expression and conveyance of the presence, life and function of the risen and living Lord Jesus Christ. Col. 1:18 - "Christ, the head of the Body the Church" I Cor. 12:12 - "members of the one Body" The physical incarnate Jesus died and rose again, and by Pentecostal outpouring indwells the collective Church as the "life-giving Spirit" (I Cor. 15:45)	Many have argued that the church is an organism, not an organization. - oftentimes such people are rebels who do not want to submit to authority. - or they may be idealists who are impractical. A church without organization will be like a formless jellyfish, and will result in social chaos.

Church

Dialectic – Both/And

Visible

Corporeal

"Body of Christ" - the visible expression of the invisible reality of the living Lord Jesus.

All that is visible and called "church" may not be the Church of Jesus Christ.

The visible church takes form in congregations of functional "members" affirming common beliefs, relating to one another in love, structurally organized for missional purposes.

These congregations may, or may not have a building to assemble in, and may or may not hold public services.

Extremism

Institutionalism
Ecclesiasticism
Incorporations: "big business"
Legal organizations
Organizational "membership"
Creedalism
Mixed membership:
Indistinguishable identification of "sheep and wolves" (Matt 7:15), "wheat and tares" (Matt. 13:29,30)
Social networking

Invisible

Incorporeal

- every individual in every time and place where-in Jesus Christ has and does live comprises the invisible Church.

The individual believers who comprise the Church are "called out" of the world and "called out" to be Christ-ones, Christians in the world.

Together they are the "holy catholic church," joined in common-unity by the presence and function of the living Lord Jesus, the "life-giving Spirit."

They are holy people "preserved" and "built up...." in Christ. (Eph. 4:12)

Extremism

Idealism
Etherealism

Ambiguous identification
- "No need to know who is, and who is not."

Universal determination
- no need for seeking to preserve unity.

Relativism
- no basis for common core beliefs.

©2014 by James A. Fowler

98

Church

Dialectic – Both/And

Extremism	Collective	Coinherence	Extremism
Collectivism	Numerous individual parts collectively comprising a whole social unit.	A unity of those in union with the living Lord Jesus Christ.	Communalism Socialism
Church viewed as aggregation - like collection of marbles in a bag.	The whole unit is only as effective as the sum of its individual parts.	A divinely established and enacted oneness of the one Body, the Church.	Interfusionism
Church viewed as conglomerate - as if glommed together with a spiritual adhesive	The ecclesial collective transcends time and space - the saints from past, present, and future.	We are in this together ... placed and put in HIM by the Grace of God.	Co-mingling
	- the saints from all races, regions, nations, gender.	Interrelational function derives from the relationality of the Triune God causing perichoretic function	Coalesence
Church viewed as congregation - just separate persons coming together in same location.	The collective of all Christ-ones ... - redeemed blood-bought children of God - regenerated by the life of Spirit of Christ.	"as one" in same space. Functional members of Body-organism; ear, eye, hand; singular function.	Important to recognize that the church involves persons in relationality.

Church

Dialectic – Both/And

← Extremism	Unity	Diversity	Extremism →
Unity is illegitimately achieved by hierarchical authority that seeks to enforce commonality, and eject, disenfranchise or excommunicate those who do not conform in thought and practice.	Integral spiritual oneness of all Christian believers "in Christ."	Christian individuals have differing personalities, talents, and opinions.	Diversity must not be allowed to degenerate in an epidemic of tolerance, whereain essential creedal unity of Christian belief is sacrificed.
Ecumenicalism Unity is not uniformity. "In essentials unity; in non-essentials liberty, in all things love."	Nicene Creed - "one holy, catholic and apostolic Church"	They tend to assemble with believers of like-minded theological opinions, worship styles, and church polity in denominationally diverse Christian groups.	Diversity must not be allowed to degenerate into divisiveness over differing thought and practice.
	I Cor 1:10 - "I exhort you.. to all agree, and there be no divisions among you"	I Cor. 12:4 - "varieties of gifts,...ministries...effects"	"Christians must agree to disagree"
	I Cor. 12:12 - "the Body is one ... one Body..."	I Cor. 12:27 - "you are Christ's Body and individually members of it"	
	Eph. 4:3,4 - "preserve unity of Spirit ... one Body"	I Cor. 12:12 - "many members, and all members are one Body"	
	Phil. 2:2 - "be of same mind,...united in Spirit"		

Artistic Expression in the Church

Dialectic – Both/And

Extremism	Showcase the Artist	Glorify God	Extremism
Tempation for egoism, pride, arrogance, narcissism, ego-trips, vanity, vain-glory - to be the center of attention, to want focus to be on them, to receive adulaton, to seek fame.	Talented individuals: - Musicians, dancers, painters, sculptors, theatrical actors, orators, etc. - Much time, effort, practice to develop quality of the art. Those occupying the stage or producing the artistic expression will inevitably receive recognition, appreciation and accolades.	Willingness and desire to take the focus and attention off of oneself in order to glorify God Genuine Christian ministry requires personal talent or adequate preparation.	Some think they are called and gifted to minister via artistic expression, but lack artistic talent or adequate preparation. - dedication and zeal for glorifying God, but without talent.
Many Christian artists have become celebrities, superstars. Often view themselves as working for Jesus or the church	- must learn to exercise their talent in humiliation that recognizes divine source of their talent. II Cor. 3:5 - "Not to consider anything as coming from ourselves"	ent to be exercised within spiritual giftedness that allows spiritual empowerment that focuses on serving others both in and outside of the Church. Requires the Christian artist to have intimate and mature relationship with the living Christ to allow the overflow of the life of Jesus unto others.	Some attempt to orchestrate a contrived form of worship. - "planned spontaneity"

Fellowship

Dialectic – Both/And

Truth	Love
Extremism	**Extremism**
	Sentimental expressions of love: - feel-good love - "ain't it nice to be nice to nice people?" Liberal activities alleged to be loving concern for others, often just to appease their own conscience and implement their own social agendas.
Christian fellowship is the interactive *koinonia* of the truth/reality of the Triune God.	Christian fellowship is the *koinonia* of the interactive loving relationality of Father, Son, & Holy Spirit
There are truth-tenets that are foundational to the Christian community. Eph. 1:13 - "the message of truth, the gospel." Col. 1:5 - "word of truth, the gospel" The Truth-person essential to Christianity is Jesus: Jn. 1:14,17 - "grace and truth realized in Christ" Jn. 8:32,36 - "the truth/the Son shall set you free" Jn 14:6 - "I am the way, the truth, and the life"	I Pet. 1:22 - "Since you have in obedience to the truth purified your souls for a sincere love of the brethren, fervently love one another from the heart." God's character of love is the relational lubrication of Christian fellowship. I Jn. 4:8,16 - "God is love" Jn. 15:10 - "abide in My love" Eph. 4:15 - "speaking the truth in love"
Extremism	
Fundamentalism - when Christian fellowship is centered around truth that is merely content of information and doctrine. Accurate data storage and consensus without Christ's relational love soon leads to divisive truth interpretations. II Jn. 1:3 - "truth and love"	

Biblical Covenants

Dialectic – Both/And

Extremism →

Extremism (Cov. Theology)	Continuity	Discontinuity	Extremism (Dispensationalist Theology)
	Promise – Fulfillment	**Old/New; Law/Grace**	

Continuity — Promise – Fulfillment

• Cov. promises Abraham
- Seed - Gen. 12:7; 13:5
- Nation - Gen. 12:2; 17:4,5
- Land - Gen. 12:7; 13:14
- Blessing - Gen. 12:2,3

• Fulfillment to Israel
- All promises fulfilled - Josh. 21:45; 23:14

• Fulfillment in Jesus
- All promises sp. fulfilled Rom. 15:8; II Cor. 1:20
- Jesus is "hope of Israel" Acts 26:6; 28:20
- Christians receive Abr. promises Gal. 3:18,29
- Spiritual Israel - Rom. 9:6; Gal.6:16

Discontinuity — Old/New; Law/Grace

• Old cov. - Mosaic Law
- First cov. II Cor. 3:14
- Israel only Ex. 34:27
- Preliminary - Heb. 8:5
- Shadow -Heb. 9:9; 10:1
- No life - Gal. 3:21

- No righteousness - Rom 3:20; Gal. 2:16,21
- Abrogated - Heb. 8:13
• New Cov. Grace/Jesus
- Second cov. Heb. 8:7;10:9
- Better cov. Heb. 7:22; 8:6
- Eternal cov. Heb. 9:15;
- Cov. of life - II Cor. 3:6
- Righteous. - II Cor. 3:19
- End of law - Rom. 10:4
- Law in hearts - Heb. 8:10
- Christians not under law Rom. 6:14,15; Gal. 3:25

Extremism (left) — Cov. Theology

- law & grace as continuity.

Law, kingdom, church viewed as continuum of re-formation.

Fear discontinuity impinges on the immutability of God.

Continued efficacy of Law - legalism, theonomy.

Fails to see radical newness of new cov. of grace.

Extremism (right) — Dispensationalist Theology

Continuity put on "hold" - resumed in future at 2nd coming for Israel

Church age never promised by God - "Plan B"

Fear continuity impinges on the promises to Israel and faithfulness of God.

Fails to see complete fulfillment in Jesus Christ.

©2014 by James A. Fowler

Eschatology – Last Things

Dialectic – Both/And

Extremism (left)

Preterism - *praeter*
Historicism - God's action past history
Contemporism - the "new age" is the "now age"
Activism - God's theocracy today
Postmillennialism
Triumphalism - "As good as it can get"
No expectation of Christ coming.
Hope is deem-phasized
Hope has become realization.
Heaven is here and now.

Already

"Last" - Acts 2:16; Heb. 1:2; II Pet. 1:20

Inaugurated eschatology - realized & experienced

Jesus Christ is the "*Eschatos* Man" – God's Last Word I Cor. 15:45

"Finished work" of Christ; *Christus Victor.* Jn. 17:4; 19:30

Not Yet

"Last" - Jn. 6:39-44; I Cor. 15:26,52; I Pet. 1:5,11; II Pet. 3:3; I Jn. 2:18

Anticipated, awaited, longed for; not yet realized.

Jesus Christ is the beginning and the end of God's work. Second coming of Christ is the consummation and completion of His redemptive work.

	Already	Not Yet
Parousia	II Peter 1:6	I Thess. 2:9; 5:21
Epiphany	Titus 2:11; 3:4	I Th. 2:8; Tit. 2:13
Manifestation	I Tim. 3:16	I Jn. 2:28; 32
Revealing	Gal. 1:16	I Pet. 1:5,7
Kingdom	Col. 1:13	I Cor. 15:24,50
Eternal life	Jn. 3:36	Jn. 6:40; Gal. 6:8
Salvation	Eph. 2:5,8	Rom. 13:11
Immortality	II Tim. 1:10	I Cor. 15:53,54

Extremism (right)

Utopianism
Apocalypticism
Millennarianism
Dispensationalism "parenthesis theory" - Plan B
Pessimism - "why polish brass on a sinking ship."
Projectionism - "pie in the sky bye and bye"
First coming of Jesus is diminished in anticipation of second.
Preoccupied with "when" & "where" of future coming.
Immortality in future.

Destiny
Dialectic – Both/And

Intentioned Universality	Conditioned Distinction
Divine intentions for mankind are always Christocentric - "in Christ." Jesus is the "Elect One," identified universally with humanity in incarnation (Phil. 2:6-8), in redemptive death (cf. Heb. 2:9), & fulfillment of all God's promises (II Cor. 1:20). II Pt. 3:9 - "God not willing that any should perish" I Tim. 2:4 - "God desires all men to be saved." Universal availability of heavenly destiny in Christ (Acts 10:34) and universal drawing of God's grace. God's determinative judgment is love "in Christ."	Volitional condition of reception or rejection, belief or unbelief. Response-ability via freedom of choice to be receptive to availability of God's salvation in Christ. Faith-receptivity of union with living Christ allows one to be "elect" in the "Elect One," Jesus Christ. Personal receptivity of faith (Jn. 3:16,36; 4:14; 11:25; Acts 10:43; I Jn 5:1). Distinct alternatives of spiritual identification and union with Christ or Satan, the perpetuity and continuity of which are heaven or hell.

← Extremism

Inevitable Universalism

- Divine imposition of destiny
  - unconditional execution of divine plan to restore and reconcile all humanity in Christ
  - All go to heaven
  - No hell
- Human "hope" of egalitarianism for all mankind.
  - no responsibility/accountability
  - unconditional

Extremism →

Necessary Dichotomy

- Divine determinism
  - double-predestination of individuals to heaven or hell by capricious divine Judge.
- Humanism
  - deems human beings to be independent selves with inherent power to make ultimate determinations.

Eternal

Dialectic – Both/And

← Extremism	Quality	Quantity	Extremism →
Religion often develops false criteria for the quality of the eternal. - the quality of the eternal is not determined by the performance efforts of humans The quality of eternality is always derivative, and nothing should be called "eternal" except that it is invested with the very presence of God.	The eternality of God's absolute character of love, justice, mercy, etc. is indicative of His unchanging Being. Eternal life - God's life - Eternal quality of the character of love and holiness Rom. 1:20 - "eternal power" Eph. 3:11- eternal purpose" II Cor. 4:17 - "eternal weight of glory" II Cor. 5:1 - "a house (body) eternal in heavens" II Thess. 2:16 - "eternal comfort and hope" Heb. 9:12 - "eternal redemption" Rev. 14:6 - "eternal gospel"	The eternality of God's Being and existence are everlasting. Ps. 90:2 - "from everlasting to everlasting You are God" Eternal life - Extension, continuity, perpetuity of divine life. Jn. 3:16,36 - "he who believes in the Son has eternal life" (cf. 5:24;6:47) Rom. 6:23 - "free gift of God is eternal life" *Aionios* applied to what is not divine, still conveys continuity, perpetuity of spiritual association. Matt. 25:41 - "eternal fire" II Thess 1:9 - "eternal destruction"	Many have been taught that the meaning of "eternal" is 'no beginning, and no end." - such an open-ended extension of time is not intrinsic to the Greek new covenant word for "eternal" (*aionios*), which means "unto the ages")

Heaven

Dialectic – Both/And

Place

Destination

Is heaven a place?

John 14:2,3 - "go to prepare a place for you" (Gk. *topos*)

Jesus speaking of heaven? Geographical? gold streets Tangible? Physical?

Ps. 18:23 - "set me in high places."

Gk *ouranos* - "raised up"

Discontinuity of worldly environ of experiencing Christ's life in physical body.

Phil. 1:21 - "to die is gain"

Rev. 21:4 - "no sorrow, pain, sickness, death"

City of the living God - Rev. 21:2, 10, 19

Person

Destiny - Consequential outcome of present reality.

Perpetuity, continuity, extension of spiritual and eternal presence of Christ.

Eph. 1:3 - "every spiritual blessing in heavenly places"

Heb. 3:1 - "partakers of a heavenly calling"

Heb. 6:4 - tasted of heavenly gift"

Matt. 10:7 - "kingdom of heaven is at hand"

Immortality, eternal life II Tim. 1:10

Perfection - eternality

Relationality

Community / fellowship

Extremism (Place)

Idealism
- clouds, harps, angels, pearly gates, mansions

Escapism -
- seeking avoidance of present-world situation.
- "can't wait 'til I get to heaven"

Mercenary
- biggest mansion
- stars in crown
- rewards

Self-oriented
- what **I** get
- what **my** body will be like
- **I** want more than **I** now have.

Extremism (Person)

Mysticism

Etherealism

"pie in the sky, bye and bye"

For some there is a discontent with what they now have in Jesus Christ, and they may be disappointed that all God has to give is His Son, Jesus Christ – in this world and the next.

Hell

Dialectic – Both/And

Place	Person
Extremism	**Extremism**
Judgmentalism	Denial of hell - "ain't no such place, and ain't nobody going there."
Some Christians seem to delight that some who have not performed as well as them are "going to fry in hell?"	Annihilationism. No after-life. After physical death, just termination and cessation of being.
Vindictive Vengeful	Universalism - Every human will inevitably go to heaven.
Hell has been misrepresented by the imagery that Dante employed in the *Inferno*.	Is hell a place of rehabilitation?

Place	Person
Destination	Destiny - consequential outcome of present reality
Is hell a place? Gk. *topos*	Continuity, perpetuity, extension of spiritual condition, association, identification, union with Satan, the Evil One.
Matt. 25:41 - *place* "prepared for the devil and his angels"	- participation in evil
Lk. 16:28- *place* of torment	- "one having power of death" - Heb. 2:14
Rev. 18:2 - "dwelling *place* of demons"	Is this forever, unending, everlasting? ...eternal?
Go into hell - Matt 5:22	Jude 13 - "forever"
Cast into hell -Mk. 9:45,47; II Pet. 2:4; Rev. 20:10	Dan. 12:2 - "everlasting contempt"
Place of fire - Mk. 9:43-48; Jude 9; Rev. 14:10	Is hell a retributory, condemnatory, sentence of guilt that incurs separation and wrath of God?
Place of destruction - Matt. 7:13; 10:28; Rom. 9:22; Phil. 3:19; I Thess. 4:3; I Tim. 6:19; I Pet. 2:3	Mt. 5:22 - "guilty .. to hell"
Discontinuity of present physical world context.	Mt. 23:33- "sentence of hell"
- "god/ruler of this world" John 12:31;14:30;II Cor. 4:4	

Judgment of God

Dialectic – Both/And

Already	Not Yet
God's judgment is God's critical determination (Greek *krisis*). - God pre-determined that His judgment would be by Jesus Christ. Jn. 5:27 - "Father gave the Son authority to execute judgment" Jn. 8:16 - "My judgment is true; I do not do it alone" Jn. 9:39 - "For judgment I came into the world" Jn. 12:30 - "judgment is upon this world; ruler of this world cast out" (16:11) Divine determination is already made for the believer who is "in Christ" Jn. 3:18 - "one who believes in Him is not judged"	Future final judgment of God based on His determination for all mankind in Jesus Christ. - Christocentric judgment Acts 10:42 - "the One appointed by God as Judge of the living and dead" Acts 17:31 - He will judge the world in righteous through a Man..." II Thess. 2:12 - all judged who did not believe in the Truth" Rom. 2:16 - "God will judge the secrets of men through Christ Jesus; Rev. 20:12,13 - "everyone judged according to their deeds"

↑ Extremism

Extremism →

Some have diminished or denied a future judgment of God - this to the detriment of advising other people that there will be consequences to their choices and actions.

Those selfishly content with their own relationship with God will be judged for their unloving unconcern for others.

Many fail to realize that God's determination for mankind is Christocentric, and that individual, subjective determination is made by one's reception or rejection of Jesus Christ.

There need be no fearful fretting about a future judgment except for those who reject Jesus.

Holy Spirit

Dialectic – Both/And

← Extremism

← Extremism

Fruit of the Spirit	Gifts of the Spirit
Character of Christ	Ministry of Christ
Gal. 5:22,23 - "the fruit of the Spirit is love, joy, peace, patience, kindness, goodness, faithfulness, gentleness, Godly control.	Rom. 12:6-8 - "gifts that differ, prophecy, service, teaching, exhortation, giving, leading, showing mercy"...
The provision by which the living Lord Jesus desires to express the character of His Being in Christian behavior.	The provision by which the living Lord Jesus desires to express the "doing" of His ongoing ministry to others in the context of His Church.
Matt. 7:16,20 - "you will know them by their fruit" "They will know we are Christians by our love" "fruit of righteousness" (Eph. 5:9; Phil. 1:11; James 3:18)	Our functionality in the local Body of Christ will be determined by our particular spiritual giftedness, and the needs of the local congregation.

Extremism (Fruit of the Spirit side):

Misunderstanding of the "fruit of the Spirit" -not plural "fruits" -complete cluster of the character of Christ in every Christian by the indwelling of Jesus.

Some identify "fruit" as the productivity of evangelism, rather than the character expression of Christ in the Christian.

Extremism (Gifts of the Spirit side):

Misuse of spiritual gifts:
- regarded as personal possessions
- considered to be trophies of spirituality.

Emphasis on supernatural activity, rather than on the divine expression of Christ's character.

Christian Baptism

Dialectic – Both/And

Extremism ←	External Act	Internal Reality	→ Extremism
Ritualism	To overwhelm with water (various modes) - visible, seen, tangible	Person's human spirit overwhelmed by the Spirit of the Triune God. (Rom. 8:9,16; I Cor. 12:13) - invisible, not seen	Metaphysical
Proceduralism	Divinely instituted action within context of Church (Matt. 28:19)		Mysticism - contact the blood of Jesus in the water?
Sacramentalism	Initiation or identificatiion as Christian?	What is the effect of water baptism on one's spiritual relationship with Jesus?	Spiritualism
Sacerdotalism - means of grace - Rite of baptism conveys, confers, causes, effects, creates or grants regeneration or salvation.	Rite of entrance into Church? ...joining the church?		Abstractionism
	Mere act of obedience?	Does the act of baptism make a person a Christian?	Etherealism
	Re-presents the imagery of the spirit overwhelmed.	Is baptism essential for salvation?	Magical
	Sacrament - visible expression of invisible reality.	- "baptized for the forgiveness of your sins" ? (Acts 2: 38)	Quietism
Pentecostalism	Spirit baptism - Tangible expression of overcoming of by the Spirit - tongues? slain in spirit? gifts of Spirit?	- "baptized into one Body" (I Cor. 12:13)	Pietism
"Wet passport"			Quakers

111

Lord's Supper

Dialectic – Both/And

Extremism →

External Act	Internal Reality
Physical rite; seen, visible, tangible activity, outward expression	Spiritual significance, meaning &/or reality; not seen, invisible
Divinely instituted/ordained activity the Church engages in repetitively. "as oft as ye do it? (1 Cor. 11:25)	"in remembrance" - (Lk. 22:19) "proclaim the Lord's death" (1 Cor. 11:26)
"first day of week" (Acts 20:7) "take eat," "drink this cup" (Matt. 26:26,27)	"the new covenant in My blood" (1 Cor. 11:25)
Physical elements of bread and fruit of the vine	"real presence of Christ" "My body...My blood" (Mk. 14:21-23)
Sacrament - visible expression of invisible reality. Re-presents in visible form the common-union (communion) of Christ and Christian), *koinonia*, participation Horizontal dimension	"eat My body, drink My blood" (Jn. 6:41-56; 1 Cor. 10:16) "What you take takes you" Mystical Body of Church - "union with Christ" (1 Cor. 6:17) Vertical dimension of worship. Mystery of participatory worship.

Extremism (External Act side):

Ritualism
Proceduralism

Sacramentalism
 - priestly confection of the sacrament.

Sacerdotalism
 - means of grace
 - the act conveys, confers, creates, causes, grants, effects the spiritual significance.

Representative
Symbolism
"Memorial meal"
"Theatre / show"
Denial of real internal effect

Extremism (Internal Reality side):

Mysticism
Spiritualism

Metaphysicalism

Esoteric

Magical

Abstractionism
Etherealism
Internalism
 - quietism, Quakers
 - pietism

Deny need of physical act

Interactive

Both/And Dialectics

of

Christian Praxis

064

Faith

Dialectic – Both/And

Initial	Continual
The initial response of faith sometimes called "saving faith" is the choice of an individual to receive the redemptive sufficiency of Christ and regenerative life of Jesus Christ. Acts 16:30 - "What must we do to be saved? Believe on the Lord Jesus Christ" Jn. 3:15,36 - "whoever believes in Him has eternal life" Acts 10:43 - "believes in Him... forgiveness of sins" Gal. 3:2 - "receive the Spirit by hearing with faith." Gal. 3:6 - "sons of God through faith in Jesus" Eph. 2:8 - "for by grace are you saved through faith"	The continuing "receptivity of Christ's activity" within the Christian life, sometimes called "living faith," is the response by which the dynamic of the living Lord Jesus' life and ministry is exprssed in Christian lives. Col. 2:6 - "as you received Jesus so walk in Him" Gal. 2:20 - "I live by faith in the Son of God." Gal. 3:11 - "the righteous man shall live by faith" II Cor. 5:7 - "we walk by faith, not sight." Col. 1:23 - "continue in faith, firmly established" Rom. 14:23 - "whatever is not from faith is sin"

Extremism (top)

Some religious groups are so focused on the "spiritual life," "deeper life," "higher life," "exchanged life," "union life," "word of faith," etc., that they neglect sharing Christ with the unregenerate.

Some have such an elitist pride in their faith that it becomes "faith in faith."

- or Gnostic

©2014 by James A. Fowler

Extremism (bottom)

Evangelical religion has often emphasized the evangelization of persons to "initial faith" in Jesus without any consequent emphasis on living by faith.

This creates churches that are filled with "babes in Christ," who do not understand what it means to be "filled with the Spirit" (Eph.5:18) unto maturity.

115

Christ-Life

Dialectic – Both/And

Extremism	Condition	Experience	Extremism
Receiving divine life often viewed as a passport to heaven. ...as merely the deposit or down-payment for what is promised in the future ...as an "end in itself", without ongoing present ramifications. It is possible to view the acquisition of Christ's life in selfish and mercenary way.	The receipt of Christ's life in spiritual regeneration, when the divine life of the Triune God comes to dwell in the spirit of a receptive individual. Rom. 8:9 - "if anyone does not have the Spirit of Christ, he is none of His" Jn. 5:24 - "passed out of death into life." Rom. 6:24 - "walk in newness of life." Exchange spiritual condition Acts 26:18 - " to turn them from darkness to light..." Col. 1:13 - "transferred to the kingdom of His Son" Receiving Christ's life by faith.	Conscious awareness of the living Christ as my life in every facet of human life, and allowing Him to live as Lord of my life. Col. 3:4 - "Christ is our life" Phil. 1:21 - "for me to live is Christ." Rom. 5:10 - "saved by His life." What is your passion, focus, *raison d'etre*? ...music, money, sports, family? Or can you honestly state, "The living Lord Jesus Christ is my *raison d'etre*, my focus, my passion, my LIFE?" Living by the life of the One who is LIFE.	Some advocate that Christians should have "constant consciousness" of Jesus - that the thought of Jesus should be on the forefront of our mind every moment. It is possible to be "so heavenly-minded, that one is of no earthly good."

Christian Life

Dialectic – Both/And

Extremism →

Impossible

"You cannot live the Christian life..."

- despite any social or religious conformity.
- despite our best efforts to self-generate and perform Christian character according to laws.

Performance - what we do, our "works," our rule-keeping in attempt to keep scriptural imperatives will not effect the Christian life.

John 15:5 - "apart from Me, you can do nothing"

I Thess. 5:24 - "He will bring it to pass"

Possible

Only the risen Lord Jesus can live the Christian life.
- He lived out the Christ-life perfectly once, and wants to do it again in us. Christian life is the re-presentation of the life and character of Jesus Christ.

Person of living Christ
- We live the Christian life by the life of Another! We derive Christian being, identity, doing, behavior from the dynamic of the living Lord Jesus via the receptivity of faith.

II Cor. 4:10 - "manifest the life of Jesus in our mortal bodies."

Extremism ↑

Escapism
- attempt to escape from all responsibility in Christian life.

Perfectionism
- "everything Jesus is and does in me is perfect, despite how it may appear to you."

↓ Extremism

Passivism
"It's His job; let Him do it!

"I am not responsible to live the Christian life, so why should I attempt to do so."
- "Just going to sit back and twiddle my thumbs until God gets into action in me"

Acquiesence

Christian Life

Dialectic – Both/And

Prescriptive	Spontaneous
What does the Christian life look like? It looks like Jesus!	When a Christian becomes a "new creature in Christ" (cf. II Cor. 5:17), that person is a unique Christ-one designed for spontaneous re-presentation of Jesus.
It is prescribed (divinely determined) by the character of Christ.	
The "how tos" of Christian living are found in the imperative requisites of the New Testament.	The indicative statements of the full provision of God's grace in Christ are the basis for spontaneous Christ-expression.
This does not mean, however, that Christians are capable by their own self-effort and performance to accomplish and maintain the living of the Christian life.	Trust that you are who you are "in Christ," and let Him BE all He wants to BE and DO in you. .
	Enjoy the Freedom. BE the unique YOU that Christ is in you.

← Extremism

Prescriptive parameters of what the Christian life should look like are often interpreted as behavioral conformity to external rules and regulations of an often authoritative "Christian law" imposed and enforced by local church leaders.

Legalism
Behaviorism

← Extremism

Some Christians interpret the freedom of being spontaneous to be a freedom to be self-serving and lawless. This can lead to a chaotic "free-for-all"

Antinomianism
Licensiousness
Libertinism

Christian Life

Dialectic – Both/And

Striving	Resting
Although "works" of human effort have no meritorious benefit to one's salvation, the outworking of the life of Jesus requires personal discipline.	Christians can "rest" from the performance of trying to please or appease God; ceasing from all works by which they might attempt to gain or enact what they already have in spiritual union with Jesus Christ, and can experience by the receptivity of faith.
Lk. 13:24 – "strive to enter through the narrow door"	Matt. 11:28 – "Come to Me, and I will give you rest."
I Tim. 4:7 – "discipline yourself unto godliness"	Heb. 4:1 – "a promise remains of entering His rest"
I Tim. 4:10 – "for this we labor and strive"	Heb. 4:3 – "we who have believed enter that rest"
Phil. 2:12 – "work out your own salvation"	Heb. 4:9 – "a Sabbath rest for the people of God"
Col. 1:29 – "I labor, striving according to His power, which mightily works within me."	Heb. 4:11 – "be diligent to enter that rest"
James 2:14,26 – "faith without works is dead"	

Extremism (left)

Performance
- Christian religion tends to approach the Christian life with constant inculcations to "measure up" to God's expectations to be holy and do right.

This "do-right" religion is allegedly effected by the self-effort ot "good works" in legalistic conformity to behavioral laws

Extremism (right)

Passivism
- some Christians have interpreted Christian rest to be a passive acquiesence that involves no responsibility or personal action.
- such a stance fails to recognize that faith is the "receptivity of divine activity," allowing Christ's life to be lived out in us.

Mysticism
Quietism

©2014 by James A. Fowler

119

Christian Life

Dialectic – Both/And

Extremism →   ← Extremism

Re-presentation	Misrepresentation
Christians are identified as "Christ-ones," who have received the living Christ as their life (Col. 3:4).	The re-presentation of the life and character of Jesus Christ necessitates the Christian's faithful receptivity of Christ's activity in the Christian life.
The purpose of the Christian life is NOT to be a representative of Jesus, doing our best to adequately be like Him. Rather, the living Lord Jesus in the Christian wants to re-present His life and character in the behavior of the Christian life.	No Christian has allowed for a perfect behavioral expression of Christ.
	I Jn. 1:8 - "if we say we have no sin, we are deceiving ourselves."
II Cor. 4:10 - "life of Jesus manifested in our bodies" Gal. 2:20 - "no longer I who live, but Christ lives in me"	Sin in the life of the Christian is a misrepresentation of one's spiritual identity; who we have become "in Christ."

Left Extremism

Perfectionism
- "I am perfect in Christ"
- "the Christian life is what the living Jesus does in me, not what I do."

Passivism
Acquiescence

Some have over emphasized identity in Christ to the point of declaring, "I am Christ."
- blasphemy

Right Extremism

Sin-consciousness
- to become too sin and Satan conscious is to fail to recognize the "finished work" and sufficiency of Jesus.
- where is our focus? on sin? or on Jesus?

Those who focus on their failure to "measure up" are focused on their own performance rather than on Person of Jesus

Truth

Dialectic – Both/And

Propositions	Person
Aristotle - "a proposition is a statement that affirms or denies a predicate of a subject."	In the metaphysics of Christian thought, truth is perceptually and spiritually invested in the divine Person of Jesus Christ.
Correspondence Theory of Truth: "A proposition is true if it corresponds with reality." - It then becomes a truth-bearing statement.	John 14:6 - "I am the way, the truth, and the life" - (the Greek word *alethia* can legitimately be translated both "truth" and/or "reality.") John 8:32 - "you will know the truth, and the truth will make you free" John 8:36 - "the Son makes you free"
Epistemological-based philosophy, theology, science, etc. The doctrine and dogma of the Church has often been cast only in the context of propositional truth.	The Truth of Jesus Christ affects people personally

Extremism

Propositions alone are static, sterile, and stagnant. - their perceived accuracy and veracity soon devolve into arguments of orthodoxy, heterodoxy, and doctrinal purity. The delimitation of reality to only naturalistic phenomenon necessarily delimits the parameters of accepted truth.	"Truth is a Person, Jesus Christ" is itself a propositional truth. When detached from the corpus of historical and theological propositional Christian truth, it can degenerate into - subjectivism - experientialism - mysticism

Christian Thought

Dialectic – Both/And

Extremism →	Objectivity	Subjectivity	← Extremism
	External history and theology	Internal "spiritual" experience	
Protestant emphasis: "as if..." righteous, mere legal fiction	Righteousness - juridical declaration of justification whereby righteous status/standing imputed.	Righteousness - Christian "made righteous" (Rom. 5:21; II Cor. 5:21) in spiritual condition in Christ.	Righteousness by correct opinion, attitudes, conformity.
Threshold factor of Christianity.	Grace - bestowed in incarnation and crucifixion	Grace - indwelling dynamic of Christ's life	Grace as booster of "infusion"
Apologetics - "Happy Birthday Jesus."	Jesus of history. Emphasis on details and application of gospel narrative.	Jesus of experience. Christ in you. Col. 1:27; Gal. 2:20; II Cor. 13:5	Postmodernism - the affect of the experience is all
Salvation as eternal commodity	Salvation - "made safe" from consequences of hell	Saving life of Christ overcoming sin inclinations.	Salvation as inner sense of wellbeing
Church as old-fashioned institution	Church - *ecclesia*, the called-out assembly in visible community.	Church - invisible reality of all Christ-indwelt persons in the "Body of Christ."	"Whoever claims to be church is church."

Human Knowledge of the Cosmos

Dialectic – Both/And

	Natural	Supernatural	← Extremism
	Science - from *scientia* - to know or perceive - observation of the physical evidence of earth origins & function. - "seeing is believing"	Biblical record of God's Self-revelation of Himself - cosmological argument of God's intelligent design of the universe. - "do not see but believe"	Supernaturalism - deny natural processes of reasoning. - Only accept what God says. - Spirit is the only reality
	Natural revelation	Special revelation	Self-limited knowledge base.
	Natural selection via the "survival of the fittest." - HOW did it form? - HOW does it change?	Teleological purpose and objective: - WHY does it exist? - Ultimate purpose?	Biblicism
	Evolution - Lat. *e*=out; *volve*=to turn or roll. - observation of how things in universe "turned out" and became as they are.	Creation - the Genesis record is accurate and regarded as being authoritative in considering origins and purpose of the cosmos glorifying God	Fideism Presupposition-alism Creationism

← Extremism

Naturalism
- reason solely on natural processes
- deny supernatural processes of reasoning.
- matter is the only reality.

Self-limited knowledge base.

Scientism

Rationalism

Empiricism
Evidentialism
Evolutionism

Knowledge
Dialectic – Both/And

Extremism	Informational	Relational	Extremism
I Cor. 8:1 - "knowledges puffs people up with pride and makes them arrogant."	Knowledge viewed from an epistemological perspective. - this is where I take my stand and assert my belief-system.	Knowledge formed by interactive discovery and interpersonal communion and intimacy. - Gen. 4:1 - "Adam knew Eve and she conceived..."	Relational knowledge when not balanced in the grounding of informational knowledge always drifts toward:
Informational knowledge when not balanced with relational knowledge always drifts toward standardization, formulization, formulization and proceduralization. - techniques and definitive determination.	A mental, rational, logical, academic, analytical approach to knowledge. Focuses on the content of information - accuracy, veracity - figured out in minds - systematically organized - consistent explanation Col. 2:8 - "elementary principles of the world"	Relational knowledge involves a person experientially and spiritually Eph. 3:19 - "to know the love of Christ which surpasses knowledge." Phil. 3:10 - "I might know Him, and the power of His resurrection" II Pet. 3:18 - "grow in the grace and knowledge of our Lord and Savior"	- subjectivism - existentialism - elitism - individualism/communalism

God's Law

Dialectic – Both/And

Extremism →

Performance Requirements

Divine prescription of performance requirements

- legal paradigm that conceives God as law-giver and Judge.
- old covenant Mosaic Law expected obedient law-keeping with consequences of blessing or cursing.

Prophecy - "I will put My law within them" (Jer 31:33)

Are there new covenant performance requirements?

Do these constitute a form of Christian law?

New covenant literature has over 1000 imperatives.

Person of Christ

Rom. 10:4 - "Christ is the end of the law for righteousness."

Rom. 13:10 - "love is the fulfillment of the law" (cf. Gal. 5:14).

Gal. 5:18 - "you are not under the Law"

Jesus Christ is the new covenant living Torah

Heb. 8:10 - "God's Law put in our minds, written in our hearts"

Gal. 6:2 - "law of Christ"
Rom. 8:2 - "law of Spirit"
James 1:25; 2:12 - "perfect law of liberty"
New covenant indicatives of grace provision.

Extremism (Antinomianism)

Antinomianism
- without prescribed parameters of performance people tend to slide toward license and libertinism.

To live only by the inner dynamic and barometer of God's grace requires the response- ability of faith.

Extremism (Legalism)

Legalism
- natural tendency of mankind to seek parameters of performance.

Romans 7 may refer to Christians operating as if moral and ecclesiastical "law" is "Christian Law."
- they will suffer the same inability and frustration as attempts to keep the Mosaic Law.

Will of God

Dialectic – Both/And

Extremism →

← Extremism

Prescription	Person
The "will of God" is viewed by many Christians as prescribed behaviors that God expects them to perform... - or a particular personal course of action (ex. marriage, vocation, etc.)	The ultimate "will of God", predestined/prehorizoned in God's intent for mankind, is each individual's reception of the Son, Jesus Christ, and living by His life in all circumstances of life.
Often viewed as: - trying to hit bullseye - finding way thru maze - puzzle to be deciphered - pleading with God to reveal His specific will	The "will of God" is always the life of the living Lord Jesus lived out in our behavior. The details are determined by the obedience of "listening under" the voice of the Spirit of Christ.
I Thess. 4:3 - "will of God, your sanctification"	
I Pet. 4:6 - "live in the Spirit according to will of God"	Mk. 4:9 - "he who has ears to hear, let him hear"

Prescription – Extremism:

All kinds of contorted procedures have been prescribed for ascertaining the supposedly elusive "will of God"

Spiritual pride leads some Christians to think they can "play Holy Spirit" in others' lives and advise them of God's will for them

Person – Extremism:

Essentialism "I am the will of God - whatever I do is the will of God for me."

Augustine - "love God and do what you want."

Spiritual pride leads some to think that they know the perfect will of God for all things at all times.

Behavioral Acceptabilities

Dialectic – Both/And

Extremism	Liberty	Limitations	Extremism
Libertarianism Libertinism License	Gal. 5:1 - It was for freedom that Christ set us free" Jn. 8:32,36 - "the Son has set us free"	Respect for others - cultural differences - religious convictions - moral weakness - personal sensitivities	Legalism - behavioral and morality codes - prohibitions - "thou shalt; thou shalt not"
Pride of liberty - flaunt, show off - shame others for non-participation.	Freedom always has a context. - Christians are free "in Christ," contextualized by His character; empowered by His grace.	Temperance Moderation	Judgmentalism - intolerance - rejective
Rom. 14:13,21; I Cor. 8:9,13 - Liberty can become stumbling-block.	Free to serve others in Christ's love. Free to do all "unto the Lord" - Rom. 14:6-8	I Cor. 8:10-13 - "Give no offense to brother" Rom. 14:20; I Cor. 8:12 - "If cause another to sin, we sin"	"Take offense" at others' liberty.
I Pet. 2:16 - "Do not use freedom as covering for evil"	Free to do all "to the glory of God" - I Cor. 10:31 Free to enjoy what God has created - I Tim. 4:4	Rom. 14:23 - "whatever is not of faith is sin" Rom. 14:13-23 - Attitudes of other Christians not infallible, but inviolable"	Impose guilt of participation and violation of what is deemed unacceptable.

Christ and the Christian

Dialectic – Both/And

"in Christ"

The Christian is incorporated into, and in union with, the living Lord Jesus I Cor. 1:30- "in Christ Jesus II Cor. 5:17 - "in Christ, ... new creature"

All that Christ IS attributed to those "in Christ"

- life (Rom. 6:23)
- salvation (II Tim 3:15)
- righteous (Phil. 3:9)
- sanctified (I Cor. 1:2)
- grace (I Cor. 1:4)
- love (Rom. 8:29)
- liberty (Gal. 2:4)
- God's will (I Thess 5:18)
- all needs (Phil. 4:19)
- complete (Col. 1:28)
- sp. blessing (Eph 1:3)
- triumph (II Cor. 2:14)
- heavenlies (Eph. 2:6)

← *Extremism*

Overly objectified detachment and separation of Christ and Christian.

Legal and forensic attribution of benefits of Christ to believer.

Such external transfer and legal imputation of Christ to the Christian diminishes the real actualization of Christ in us.

"Christ in you"

The Spirit of the living Lord Jesus enters into the spirit of receptive believer Rom. 8:16 - "Spirit bears witness with our spirit" Gal. 2:20 - "no longer I, but Christ lives in me."
Col. 1:27 - "Christ in you, the hope of glory"
II Cor. 13:5 - "Jesus Christ is in you, unless you believed in vain"
Eph. 3:17 - "Christ dwells in your hearts"
Rom. 8:10,11 - "Christ in you ... dwells in you"
Not just indwelling location for personal benefit
- Christ in you as your life
- Christ in you as love for others

← *Extremism*

Overly subjectified immanence and identification of Christ and Christian.

Monism
Pantheism
- inordinate merging or mingling or absorption of Christ and the Christian that fails to preserve distinction.

"I am Jesus Christ in my form"

©2014 by James A. Fowler

Christ and the Christian - Ontological Union

Dialectic – Both/And

Extremism	Spirit-union of Being	Personal distinction	Extremism
Essential union of Christian & Christ -absorbed, fused, equivalence, monistic merging. - Christian one with Christ -Christian deified Union is lost in "oneness"	The Christian is joined in a one-spirit union with the Spirit of Christ.	Christ and the Christian individual remain distinct personages.	Deistic detachment, separation from God. Transcendence; no immanence. - God's up in heaven; I am here on earth."
	I Cor. 6:17 - "he who is joined to the Lord is one spirit with Him." Gal. 2:20 - "no longer I live, but Christ lives in me" II Pt. 1:4 - "partaker of the divine nature"	Rom. 8:16 - "Spirit bears witness with our spirit, that we're children of God Gal. 2:20 - "Christ lives in me ... the life I now live in the flesh I live by faith..."	
Humanity is de-personalized. - obliteration, annhilation, displacement, replacement - "I am no longer human. - "I am not; only He is."	Col. 3:3,4 - "our life hid with Christ in God. Christ is our life" Eph. 1:3 - "every spiritual blessing in heavenly places in Christ Jesus." Eph. 2:6 - "seated in the heavenly places in Christ Jesus"	I Jn. 4:12-16 - "God in us" Col. 1:27 - "Christ in you" Rom. 8:11 - Holy Spirit indwells you"' Distinction of "yourself" Rom. 6:11,13; II Tim 2:15 We retain personal individuality and humanity.	Self-deprecating, self-denigrating view of humanity - "just a sinner saved by grace." Double-minded - schizophrenic concept of dual natures.

Christ and the Christian - Operational Union

Dialectic – Both/And

Extremism	Union of doing	Personal distinction	Extremism
Inevitable expression of Christ. - "All that I do is Christ in action." - "Christ is the new man in me; Christ cannot sin; I can't sin." - "Do what you will; for what you will is what He wills." - "God does not mean for man to have faith; just to be the God expresser that he is" - "just go with the flow"	Grace dynamic of divine activity. - Jesus is the dynamic of all His demands. II Cor. 12:9 - "My grace is sufficient for you" II Cor. 9:8 - "God able to make all grace abound" Phil. 2:13 - "God is at work in us" I Thess. 5:24 - "He will bring it to pass" II Cor. 3:5 - "our adequacy is of God" II Cor. 4:10,11 - "life of Jesus manifested in us" Gal. 5:16,25 - "live / walk by the Spirit" Rom. 15:18 - "Christ accomplished through me"	Response-ability: Christians make faith choices of behavior. Jn. 15:5 - "Apart from Me, you can do nothing." Phil. 4:13 - I can do all things through Christ." Faith - our receptivity of His activity. Rom. 1:5 - "obedience of faith" James 2:12-26 - "faith without works is useless" Rom. 14:23 - "whatever is not of faith is sin" Phil. 2:12 - "work out your own salvation; God is at work in you."	False religious idea of self-generated righteous behavior. - "God helps those who help themselves." - Do your best, and God will do the rest." Religious attempts at commitment and dedication to live Christian life. Trying to "be like Jesus." - imitation, following His example.

Christian

Dialectic – Both/And

← Extremism   Perfect   Sinful   Extremism →

Perfectionism (Extremism)	Perfect	Sinful	Perpetual Sinful Depravity (Extremism)
Perfectionism	Spiritual condition - derived nature & identity	Behavioral patterning in soul and body.	Perpetual sinful depravity of all human beings due to Fall of mankind in Adam.
Holiness Movement - "Entire Sanctification" - Christian is not sinful; has no sin - redefine sin as mistakes.	Perfect - Heb. 10:14 - "perfected those sanctified" Holy - "saints - holy ones" Rom. 1:7 - "called saints" Righteous M. Luther - "*simul iustus et peccator*" - simultaneously justified and sinful.	I John 1:8 - "if we say we have no sin, we are deceiving ourselves and the truth is not in us" "Flesh" patterns of selfishness and sinfulness in the desires of our soul.	- humanity is inherently and essentially sinful - depraved, deficient, defective, damned.
"Made righteous" thought to mean: - inherently and essentially righteous - "I am righteous" *a se*, in myself.	- Not just "declared righteous," but "made righteous" - I Cor. 1:30 - "Christ became to us righteousness" Spiritual - Gal. 6:1 - "you who are spiritual" Godly - II Pt. 2:9	Gal. 5:16 - "desires of the flesh" Gal. 5:17 - "flesh sets its desires against Spirit" Eph. 2:3 - "desires of the flesh" II Pt. 2:18 - "fleshly desires" Rom. 7:17,20 - "sin indwells me"	A Christian is just a "sinner saved by grace." - saved by "alien righteousness" of Jesus.

Christian Behavior

Dialectic – Both/And

Triumphalism

- "Since the Spirit of Christ lives in me, and He does not sin, I don't have to worry about sinning."
- "Whatever I do is Christ working in me."

Perfectionism

- "those of us who are 'spiritual' do not have to concern ourselves with the 'deeds of the flesh.'"

©2014 by James A. Fowler

Flesh	Spirit
New covenant understanding of "flesh" recognizes the patterning of the desires of the soul into selfish and sinful propensities	The Spirit of Christ dwells within the spirit of every Christian person.
	Rom. 8:9 - "if any one does not have the Spirit of Christ, he is none of His"
Eph. 2:3 - "desires of the flesh"	Rom. 8:16 - "the Spirit bears witness with our spirit that we are children of God."
II Pt. 2:10 - "the flesh with its corrupt desires."	
Gal. 5:17 - "the flesh sets its desires against the Spirit"	Gal. 5:17 - "the Spirit *sets its desires* against the flesh"
"Flesh" seeks to "act out" in expression of selfish character in our behavior.	The Spirit desires to express its fruit-character in Christian behavior.
Gal. 5:19-21 - "the deeds of the flesh are immorality, impurity, sensuality, strife, jealousy, anger …"	Gal. 5:22,23 - "fruit of the Spirit is love, joy, peace …"
	Phil. 1:11 - "fruit of righteousness"

Defeatism

- "Just a sinner, saved by grace"
- "Just a carnal (fleshly) Christian"
- "I can't help but sin, I'm only human."
- "It's just my human nature."

Activism

- Attempts to live the Christian life by self-effort.
- trying to be "like Jesus"
- Flesh attempts to imitate Jesus.

Work of Christ in Christian

Dialectic – Both/And

	Dealing with Sin	Victory in Christ	
Extremism ←			→ **Extremism**
Dealing with sin by religious self-effort	Indwelling sinfulness - sin indwells - Rm 7:17-20 - not perfect - Phil. 3:12 - confess sins - I Jn. 1:8,9	Indwelling Christ - Christ in you - Col. 1:27 - More than conquerors in Christ - Rom. 8:27	Claiming oneness with God, without sin
"Just a sinner saved by grace"	Christ as Savior	Christ as Lord	"Everything Christ is, I am"
Activism "Do your best" Moralism "Do-right religion" Legalism "Do this, do that"	Soul action - "good that I would, I do not" - Rom. 7:16,19 - "flesh" patterned desires against Spirit - Gal. 5:17	Spirit action - "led by the Spirit" Rom. 8:14; Gal. 5:18 - "Spirit sets its desires against flesh" - Gal. 5:17	Triumphalism "What I do is what He does" Perfectionism "We do not sin" Mysticism spiritual knowers "we have arrived"
Confessionalism "So sorry, Lord"	Process *negativa* - "be not conformed to this world" - Rom. 8:2 - Cross - (experiential) - Repentance "I can't; only He can"	Process *positiva* - conformed to the image of His Son" - Rom. 8:29 - Resurrection life - All sufficiency in God's Grace - II Cor. 9:8	
Hypocrisy "Carnal Christian" "Two natures" fallacy			Antinomianism - freedom pushed to extreme.

082

©2014 by James A. Fowler

133

"Inner Man" of Christian

Dialectic – Both/And

← Extremism	Spirit	Soul	Extremism →
Sp. Perfectionism Full Sanctification Sinlessness Eradicationism	Spiritual condition - Spiritual exchange Acts 26:18 - Indwelling Trinity - Indwelling function of Father, Son, Holy Spirit	Behavioral function - Choosing creatures - Faith choice - Col 3:2 - Response-ability	Sp. Positionalism - legal declaration of status w/ God - adjudicated righteousness
Supersessionism - I am replaced by Christ - "Everything I do is Christ in me"	Spiritually new - II Cor. 5:17 - New man - Eph. 4:24	Behavioral conflict - Flesh & spirit - Gal. 5:17 - Desire to do good - Sin indwells - Rom. 7:17 Behavioral imperfection - Phil. 3:12	Two naturism - schiophrenic - paranoid uncertainty
Spiritual pride Gnostic elitism Union with Christ taken to extreme of essentialism. - uni-naturism	Spiritual completeness - All sp. blessings - Eph 1:3 - All things - I Co. 2:21-23 Spiritual union - I Cor 6:17 Spiritual nature - II Pt 1:4 Spiritual sufficiency - Grace - II Cor. 9:8 - Strength - Eph. 3:16	Behavioral inability - no sufficiency- II Cor. 3:5 - can do nothing - Jn 15:5 Behavioral formation - transformed - Rom. 12:2 - conformed - Rom. 8:29 - Christ formed - Gal 4:19	Suppressionism - trying to suppress sin in order to be righteous. Legalism Moralism Performance-oriented
Mysticism Libertinism	Sp. perfection - Phil. 3:15 Mind of Christ - I Co. 2:16	Behavioral salvation -saved by His life - Rm. 5:10 Renew mind - Rom. 12:2	

Church Growth

Dialectic – Both/And

Quantitative

The Church is always concerned that others are introduced to life and hope in Jesus Christ, and thus added to the community of faith, the Church.

Acts 2:41 - "added about three thousand souls"

Acts 5:14 - "multitudes of men and women added"

The Church is the assembly of Christ-indwelt persons that is difficult to identify and quantify.

Those who profess faith and occupy a pew are not necessarily Christ-ones.

Qualitative

Christian thought begins with the character of the Holy God and is directed toward the manifestation of divine character in the behavior of Christians.

A major objective of the Church is to explain the dynamic of God's grace to express the character- "fruit of the Spirit" (Gal. 5:22,23)..

I Pet. 2:2 - "grow in respect to salvation"

II Pet. 3:18 - "grow in the grace and knowledge of Lord Jesus."

Eph. 1:4 - "be holy"

Extremism (Quantitative):

Evangelism is inordinately emphasized by some as they seek to:
- build empires
- megachurches
- political power-bases

Church growth techniques:
- programs
- publicity
- fundraising

Numerical, statistical success factors:
- buildings
- budgets
- baptisms

Extremism (Qualitative):

Pietism
- an emphasis on external behavior that often leads people to become "fruit-inspectors" of one another's behavior.

Some groups of Christians become in-grown, preoccupied with their own "spirituality"
- "faithful few"
- "Holy Club"
- remnant of the loyal

135

Discipleship

Dialectic – Both/And

Instructional	Relational
The discipleship process of bringing believers to maturity in Christ will inevitably involve the didactic instruction of doctrinal information.	The relationality of the Triune Father, Son and Holy Spirit necessitates that we introduce Christians to an intimate relationality with God and with other Christians in the Church.
The *Didache*, a late 1st or early 2nd century Christian document, was an early catechismal teaching or discipleship manual.	It seems best to meet a fellow believer where they are in life, and allow their questions to direct the relation and conversation. - introducing them to the personal relationality of prayer, worship, and devotional life. - encouraging them in the "one another" emphases of scripture.
All believers need to have a basic knowledge of the teachings of the Church, as well as the biblical narrative and its interpretation.	

Extremism

Some regard the Church to be primarily an educational institution for the transmission of Christian information.

Knowledge, even Christian knowledge can foster arrogance (cf. I Cor. 8:1)

Christianity is not intended to be a mere "believe-right" religion.

Extremism

It is possible to so emphasize the relationality of Christian "community" and fellowship that basic Christian instruction is neglected.

Relationality can become a fuzzy, feel-good comradery that fails to maintain any content or direction in building "disciple" of the living Lord Jesus.

Mission of the Church

Dialectic – Both/And

← Extremism	Truth	Love	Extremism →
	Christocentric Truth Jn. 14:6 - "I AM ... Truth"	Christocentric Love I Jn. 4:8,16 - "God is love"	
Evangelism - popularly perceived as proceduralized techniques, formulas for sharing basic content of gospel. - 4 spiritual laws	The "truth of the gospel" - Gal. 2:5,14; Eph. 1:13; Col. 1:5 - gospel, *euangellion*, "good news"	Loving relational fellowship of Christian people should be attractive to those in rejective fallen world.	Socialism Communalism - all-inclusive loving community -"all are welcome -"it doesn't matter what you believe," - "we love all"
	Content of gospel	Compassion for people	
Ideological data transmission - didacticism - fundamentalism - catechism	St. Francis - "Share Christ wherever you go, and if necessary use words."	"They'll know we are Christians by our love"	Relativism - "everyone allowed to have their own truth"
	Jesus Christ is the Truth, the reality, that every person needs to know.	Jesus Christ is present in every Christian for the purpose of expressing His LOVE to OTHERS.	
Conservatism - believe-right religion. - epistemology	Eph. 4:15 - "speak the truth in love"	II Jn. 1:1 - "love in truth"	"Ain't it nice to be nice to nice people?"

Identity

Dialectic – Both/And

	Psychological	Spiritual	Extremism
Physicalism	Identity often based on physical criteria: - photographs - fingerprints - eye mapping	Internal and invisible sense of identity based on spiritual identification at the very core of our human being.	Abstractionism
Humanism	Personal sense of identity often based on: • physical characteristics and abilities; ...beauty, intelligence,	I Jn. 3:10 - "children of God, children of devil obvious"	Spiritual pride
Performance	personality, athletic prowess, sexual prowess, musical ability, vocational career	Spiritual identity is determined by our spiritual union with spirit-being, and thus a derived spiritual nature.	Perfectionism.
Materialism	• physical possessions; ...houses, cars, portfolios, clothing, furniture	Derived spiritual identity. The basis of who I am is who He is!	
Associationism	• personal associations; ... sororities, fraternities, social organizations, church attended	Christian identity is not based on fleshly tendencies in one's soul	Blasphemy of claiming to be who He alone is. - "I am Jesus Christ..." - "I am the Holy Spirit..."
Religionism		We are not just "sinners saved by grace."	

Extremism

Freedom

Dialectic – Both/And

	Extremism	FROM	TO	Extremism
License		Freedom from sin - Rom. 6:7,18,22; 8:2	Free to "live by the Spirit" - Rom. 8:2	Spiritualism
Libertinism		Freedom from "flesh" - Gal. 5:17	Free to manifest "fruit of the Spirit" - Gal. 5:22,23	
Libertarianism		Freedom from Law - Rom. 7:3; 8:2,3; Gal. 5:1-13	Free to live in context of eternity - Phil. 3:20	Futurism
Antinomianism				
Sinlessness		Freedom from Death - Rom. 8:2; Heb. 2:15	Free to live in hope - Col. 1:27	Escapism
Anti-religionism		Freedom from Religion - Col. 2:20-23	Free to glorify God - I Cor. 10:20	
		Free from guilt	Free to doubt	Skepticism
		Free from fear	Free to rest/relax	Lethargy
		Free from "trying to live the Christian life"	Free to live spontaneously	
		Free from correctness	Free to be your unique and different self	Individualism
		Free from living by other's expectation	Free to live without demanding any "rights"	
		Free from habituated behavior patterns	Free to be alone - with God	Monasticism
			Free to live for others	

Holiness

Dialectic – Both/And

Spiritual Condition	Behavioral Expression
When the "Holy One," Jesus Christ (Acts 3:14; 7:52; 13:35), by the Spirit, indwells the spirit of a receptive individual, that person has a spiritual condition of holiness and is identified as a "holy one," saint.	The indwelling presence of the Holy One is intended to progressively manifest His holy character in the behavior of His holy people.
Eph. 1:4 - "holy and blameless before Him"	I Pet. 1:16 - "be holy,...for I am holy"
Col. 3:12 - "holy and beloved"	II Cor. 1:12 - "in holiness and godly sincerity we have conducted ourselves."
Eph. 4:24 - "new self ... created in righteousness and holiness of the truth"	II Cor. 7:1 - "perfecting holiness in the fear of God"
Eph. 5:27 - "church ... holy and blameless"	II Pt. 3:11 - "holy conduct and godliness"
Heb. 3:1 - "holy brethren"	Heb. 12:10 - "that we might share in His holiness"
I Pet. 2:9 - "holy nation"	Heb. 12:14 "holiness without which no man shall see the Lord"

← Extremism

Derived spiritual condition of saint or "holy one" does not imply essential holiness of character.

"God is holy" essentially holy *a se*, in Himself, but a Christian identified as a "holy one" is not essentially holy, but derives holy condition and expression from the holy character of God.

← Extremism

Pietistic holiness - conformity to behavioral, clothing, worship patterns deemed to be "holy"

External holiness expressions do not create or constitute internal spiritual condition of holiness.

Christian holiness (condition and expression) is always derived holiness.

Love

Dialectic – Both/And

Extremism	Personal Act	God's Character	Extremism
Activism - active gestures of compassionate benevolence, whether individual or collective, may be admirable, but if not derived out of the divine *agape* love of God's character, do not qualify as Christian love. - may be merely sentimentalism and affection.	Many imperatives calling on Christians to "love" in new covenant. - "love one another" (Jn. 13:34,35; 15:12,17; Rom. 13:8) - "love neighbor" (Matt 22:39; Mk 12:31) - "love enemies" (Matt. 5:44; Lk 6:27,35) - "love wives" (Eph. 5:25,28; Col. 3:19) - "love husbands" (Titus 2:4) I Jn 4:12 - "if we love one another, God abides in us, and His love is perfected in us."	I Jn. 4:8,16 - "God is love" - this is the indicative on which all imperatives for personal love action is predicated. Divine *agape* love can only be expressed in human behavior as it is spiritually derived from God. Rom. 5:5 - "the love of God poured out in our hearts by Holy Spirit given to us. Rom. 15:30 - "love in the Spirit" Gal. 5:22 - "the fruit of the Spirit is love ..."	**Passivism** - No such reality as "passive love" - love is always actively expressed toward others. I Jn. 4:8 - "the one who does not love does not know God." I Jn. 4:20 - "the one who does not love his brother whom he has seen, cannot love God whom he has not seen."

Sexuality
Dialectic – Both/And

Extremism →	External Act	Internal Perspective	Extremism →
Perfunctory sex Mechanical sex Casual sex Focus on sexual performance or frequency. Sexual immorality - fornication - adultery - promiscuity - prostitution - rape, incest - voyeurism - sadism - sexual abuse - polygamy - persons used as sex objects	"Sex" from Lat. *sexus* - "to divide." Gen. 1:27 - "male & female He created them" Gen. 1:28 - "be fruitful and multiply" Gen. 2:25 - "naked and not ashamed" Gen. 2:24 - "be one flesh" Intercourse between man and woman. - Greek *koite* - get Eng. word "coitus" Heb. 13:4 - "let marriage bed (*koite*) be undefiled" Genital friction of male penis glans/female clitoris leading to climax. Masturbation? Homosexuality	• Psychological – - mental thought life is important component of human sexuality. - emotional feelings are present in sexual acts - volitional choices of sexual involvement. • Spiritual – God created sexuality and sustains its beauty. Gal. 3:28 - "male & female, one in Christ Jesus" I Pt. 1:7 - "fellow heirs of grace of life" Every act of Christian life, an act of worship. Christ in Christian engages in sexual expression. Character of Christ in every sexual action.	Sexual addiction, obsession, compulsion - lust, fantasizing - sexual fetishes Pornography - visual images used as substitute for physical act, or as virtual reality/vicarious experience. Religious deification of sexual actions. - Aphrodite - Venus

Marriage
Dialectic – Both/And

Union	Distinction
Gen. 2:24 - "they become one flesh"	Unique personalities of husband and wife. They remain individuals, not lesser or superior to other.
Mal. 2:15 - "God made one"	
Matt. 19:6 - "what God has joined, let no man part asunder"	Marriage designed for complementarity.
Two become one in spirit, soul and body.	Love requires "other" to be love.
Spiritual union - I Cor. 7:39 I Pet. 3:7	Interactive communication of ideas, values, interests.
Covenant union - Mal. 2:14 Prov. 2:17	- marital love involves enjoying the differences.
Legal union - divinely ordained institution	- working through situations in harmony and reconciliation.
Love union - seeks highest good of the other	Maintaining distinction requires respect of the other's ideas and interests in transparency, honesty and integrity.
Relational union - mutual interdependence	
Physical, sexual union - Heb. 13:4 - marriage bed	

Extremism (Union side)

- Essential Union Union of partners pushed to point of fusion, absorption, or "couplism"
  - separate identity disallowed. Other partner regarded as "my life."
  One regarded as extension of other.
- Authoritarianism Ownership or controlling of the other. Disallowing of differences.

Extremism (Distinction side)

Individualism
- selfish pursuits
Gender wars
-male chauvinism
-feminist agenda
Competition
Role-playing
Detachment
- co-habitants
- separation and divorce
Hidden secrets
- deceit, manipulation, addiction, false accusations, sexual liasons
Selfishness
-narcissism
-self-gratification

Marriage

Dialectic – Both/And

Extremism →	Divine Order	Mutual Deference	← Extremism
Hierarchialism Authoritarianism - husband not to be a dictator, boss - wife not to be subservient slave.	Respect for God's design Divine institution of marriage has order.	Respect for spouse Love, honor, esteem allows one to trust & yield to other, not demanding our own agenda and interests.	Egalitarianism Libertarianism
"Control issues" in marriages. Demand for submission evidences inequality.	Matt. 19:5,6 - "leave father and mother, joined to wife as one flesh"	Eph. 5:21 - "have deference for one another"	Laissez faire - indifference - dispassionate - "whatever!" - "who gives a damn?"
No excuse for rudeness, selfishness, intimidation, fear	Eph. 5:22,25 - "wives be subject to husbands; husbands love your wives. Col. 3:18 - "wives be subject to your husbands." I Pet. 3:1 - "wives be submissive to own husbands"	Phil. 2:3,4 - "Do nothing from selfishness ... regard the other as more important than yourselves; .."	When a couple is overly deferential it produces disordered interpersonal relationship, with frustration and resentment.
Biblical statements regarded as rules or role-playing.	Divine order: Equality of husband and wife - cf. Gal 3:28 Christ in you as husband. Christ in you as wife.	Love seeks highest good of the other, willing to limit my freedom to grant freedome to the other. Free... ..from performance ..to have opinions, interests ..to develop personality ..to follow dreams	

Marriage

Dialectic – Both/And

Extremism	Work	Grace	Extremism
Legalism - "God's rules for a happy marriage" - "live by the Book and you will please God."	Marriage takes more than love – it takes hard work! Love is always active. Marriage is responsibility.	You cannot make your marriage work! Marriage is impossible by our best self-effort.	Defeatism "If you can't make it work, leave it and try another."
Absolutism of thinking that one has marriage all figured out. - "Religion has destroyed more marriages than it has helped."	Imperatives of marrage: – "love your wives" - Eph. 5:25,28; Col. 3:19; I Pt 3:7 - love husbands" Tit. 2:4 - "wives submit to husbands" - Eph. 5:24; Col. 3:18,19; I Pet. 3:1 - respect husb. Eph 5:33	Indicative of resource and provision for marriage: - The grace-dynamic of the living Lord Jesus Christ Gal 5:22,23 - Fruit of the Spirit	Abstractionism - Can't get a handle on grace"
	Love is not something we can generate and enact. Decision of faith to allow love to function in us	Love is the character of the Triune God. "God is love" - I Jn. 4:8,16 "love of Christ controls us" - II Cor. 5:14 "faith thru love" - Gal 5:6	Relativism - Traffic on grace, by turning the provision of grace into narcissistic selfishness.
Hypocrisy of thinking marriage is accomplishment - "marriage is what you make it"	Role of husband - head Role of wife - subservient	Christ in you as husband. Christ in you as wife.	Passivism - "Just go with the flow of grace"

145

Family

Dialectic – Both/And

Extremism (Social Unit)	Social Unit	Individuals	Extremism (Individuals)
Deification of family relationships and loyalty.	Family is a divinely instituted microcosm of social community.	A family is comprised of individuals with differing ages, genders, and personalities.	Individualism - "I don't need others to be who I am!"
Authority structures often become the primary format and dynamic of family interactions. - often leads to abuse of authority	Relational function of family based on Triune interrelations of love.	Each individual has unique "way he should go" (Prov. 22:6).	Absence of any sense of family loyalty.
Gothard emphases - perpetual paternal authority - umbrella of authority	Biblical model of family: Husband, wife, children Eph 5:24-33 - "husbands/wives (Col. 3:18,19) Eph. 6:1-4 - "children/parents" (Col. 3:20,21) Exod 20:12 - "honor your father and mother"	Individuals must learn to relate to others in love and deference, with respect, honor and obedience for God-ordained authority. - such relations should not take advantage of others in ways that provoke, exasperate, or lead to "disputes, dissensions, or outbursts of anger" (Gal. 5:20).	Excessive emphasis on personal independence.
	Opportunities to learn: - how Trinity functions - how to fail, be accepted - basis of forgiveness. - that authority is intrinsic to all social units. - how to accept discipline	Relationship of individuals supersedes authority.	Undue emphasis on personal "rights" or privileges.

Counseling

Dialectic – Both/And

Behavioral Advice	Spirit-counsel	Spiritualism
Instruction and suggestion for regulation of human behavior.	The Spirit of Christ is the ultimate counselor:	"spirituo-therapy" - principles and procedures of how the Spirit allegedly works in various situations.
Such "counsel" includes:	Isa. 9:6 – "Counselor..."	
- moral advice	Jn. 14:16,26; 15:26; 16:7 "send counselor, Spirit."	
- psychological principles	I Cor. 3:18 – "the Lord, the Spirit.	
- biblical principles and imperatives (though often disconnected from indicatives of God's provision).	I Cor. 15:45 – "last Adam, life-giving Spirit"	Some who think they have "gift of counseling," are just trying to "play Holy Spirit" in the lives of others.
- "how-tos" - avoid temptation, pray, read bible, personal examples; sharing what has happened in one's own life	The pneumatic Christ is the Spirit-counselor.	
Rom. 15:14 – "competent to counsel" (Jay Adams)	Spirit-counsel is sharing Christ in a way that another person can personally relate the living indwelling Christ to their situations of life.	
- nouthetic counseling	Eph. 1:11 – "the counsel of His will"	
- cognitive counseling		
- behavioral counseling		

Psychologism
- unending stream of theories of how to live in one's own strength
- psycho-therapy

Humanism

Behaviorism
- advocacy of self-effort techniques for self-regulation of one's behavior.

Job's counselors:
Job 26:3,4;
Job 38:2;
Job 42:9

Forgiveness

Dialectic – Both/And

← Extremism	Divine Source	Human Conduit	Extremism →
Claiming inability of natural forgiveness, saying, "Only God can forgive," can be an avoidance of responsibility. - unwilling to be the conduit of relational forgiveness. The Church is the society of the forgiven, but must not be a cluster of "forgiven sinners" longing for heaven and fail-- ing to express forgiveness.	Triune God is the relational source of all genuine forgiveness: - Only God can forgive the wrongdoing that is contrary to His character - His forgiveness based on His character of LOVE revealed in the incarnation and death of His Son Divine forgiveness of sin is received by faith. A Christ-one (Christian) has received Jesus, the eternal Forgiver to dwell within and be the Life-expression in him/her. It is incongruous that a Christian should say, "I just can't forgive myself."	The relational forgiveness of others who might have wronged us is predicated on receiving God's forgiveness. The indwelling presence of the Divine Forgiver provides the Christian with everything necessary to forgive others. The Christian becomes the conduit of God's divine forgiveness, allowing such forgiveness to flow to others despite how we might have been wronged, and without any residual resentment or bitterness. Unforgiveness has consequences - Ps. 132:1-4	Non-acceptance of God's forgiveness expressed by us places the onus on the one who has thus "taken offense." Failure to recognize the indwelling presence of the Divine Forgiver in the Christian casts the believer into increased religious self-effort to muster up a forgiving attitude

Christian Giving

Dialectic – Both/And

Extremism	Proportional	Personal	Extremism
Legalism	Tangible assets are given:	Divine Giver (Father, Son, and Holy Spirit) lives in the Christian.	Idealism
II Cor. 9:7 - under comulsion"	I Cor 16:2 - " as God has prospered."	Intangible assets of God's grace via Jesus Christ.	- many pragmatic realists cannot conceive that giving by the grace-prompting of God's Spirit will ever adequately finance the Church and what God might want to do in today's world.
Legislated and mandated percentages - tithing	II Cor. 8:11,12 - "according to what we have"	- James 1:17 - " every good gift is from above."	
Ecclesiasticism	God not interested in our tangible gifts until we first give ourselves to Him - II Cor. 8:5	- Rom. 8:32 - "freely gives us all things"	
Hitting people up for contributions for projects.	Then we respond to the overflow of God's abundance:	God's grace expressed in our givingness- II Cor. 8:1	"just pie in the sky bye and bye"
Christian giving is NOT:	Eph. 2:7 - "riches of grace"	Freedom of choice to give	
- guilt-motivated	II Cor. 8:7 - "abound in everything"	II Cor. 8:3 - "our accord"	
- need-actuated	"If given much, much required" - Lk. 12:48	II Cor. 9:7 - "as they purposed in their hearts"	
- manipulated	Purposed and planned calculation of tangible giving.	"God loves a cheerful/satisfied giver" (II Cor 9:7)	
- to repay God		By obedience we "listen under" God's direction to determine what/to whom He would have us to give.	
- giving beyond our means			
- for prosperity			
- for glory of man			
- for tax purposes			

Obedience

Dialectic – Both/And

	Keeping commands	Listening to God	
Extremism			**Extremism**

Listening to God

The new covenant (New Testament) concept of obedience is based on the Greek *hupakouo* meaning "to listen under."
- relational *koinonia* with Triune God.
- listen under God's voice to ascertain His direction of what He desires to do and be in our lives.

Obedience of faith (Rom. 1:5; 16:26)
- listening under God, the Christian responds with receptivity to His activity.

I Pt. 1:2 – "to obey Jesus Christ"

Acts 5:29 – "obey God rather than man"

Keeping commands

Particularly in the old covenant (Old Testament) obedience was conceptualized in terms of keeping the rules and regulations of the Mosaic Law
- Deut. 27:10 - "obey God and do His commands"
- Judges 3:4 - "obey the commandments..."

New Covenant advocates respect for authority

I Pt. 2:13 - "submit to every human institution ... one in authority."

Heb. 13:7 - "obey leaders"

I Pt. 3:6 - "Sarah obeyed Abraham"

Eph. 6:1 - "obey parents"

Extremism (Listening to God side):

Passivism
- to listen with no intent to respond to what one is told is but an exercise in futility.

The familiar hymn advocates that we "Trust and Obey"
- to affirm one's trust in God's love and faithfulness without consequent obedient listening is hypocrisy.

Extremism (Keeping commands side):

Legalism
- when obedience is conceived only as commandment-keeping, it will inevitably be performance-based self-effort to keep religious or social laws.

Unquestioned obedience to authority allows tyranny to thrive.

Cross of Christ

Dialectic – Both/And

	Historical Event	Personal Implications	
Extremism Historicism Evangelical Christianity has often emphasize the objective historical event to the neglect of the subjective personal and experiential implications. View Christianity - as historical society - as theological society	Heinous travesty of justice when Jewish religious leaders and the Roman authorities acted in concert to orchestrate the murderous execution of an innocent individual. (cf. Acts 4:27; Objective - external, outside of ourselves. I Cor. 15:3 - "Christ died for our sins" Rom. 5:8 - "while yet sinners, Christ died for us" I Cor. 1:23 - "we preach Christ crucified" I Cor. 1:28 - "crucified the Lord of glory" I Pt 3:18 - "Christ died for sins once for all"	More than just a parochial execution, the death of Jesus on a Roman cross was God's means to overcome spiritual death and effect the death of the "old man" in those individuals who receive Jesus' life. Subjective - internal, inside of ourselves. Rom. 6:2 - "died to sin" Rom. 6:6 - "old man has been crucified with Christ" Gal. 2:20 - "I have been crucified with Christ..." Col. 2:20 - "you have died with Christ" II Tim. 2:11 - "if we died with Him, we also shall live with Him"	**Extremism** Experientialism Crucifixionism - Some Christians emphasize "dying to self" or self-crucifixion as a self-effort performance requirement of the Christian life. Although mortification of our sinful behaviors is part of Christian life, this is to be work of Spirit, not self-effort.

©2014 by James A. Fowler

Resurrection

Dialectic – Both/And

Event	Dynamic
Historical events are necessarily static.	Risen and living Lord Jesus is dynamic.
Individual physical Christ Jesus was put to death on the cross, and on the third day was raised from the dead.	Risen Lord Jesus continues to live as the pneumatic Christ who raises spiritually dead individuals to newness of life.
Information	Transformation
John 20:1 - "stone rolled away from the tomb." Lk. 24:12 - "Peter saw the linen wrappings" I Cor. 15:4 - "He was raised on the third day..." I Cor. 15:14 - "If Christ not raised, preaching/faith is vain."	Rom. 6:4 - " newness of life" Phil. 3:10 - "know the power of the resurrection" Rom. 1:4 - "Son of God w/ power by resurrection." I Cor. 15:45 - "last Adam became life-giving Spirit" I Pt 1:3 - "born again... through the resurrection"

← Extremism

Historicism

The Christian faith is more than just an historical society to remember the events of Jesus' life.

Theologism

The Christian faith is more than just a theological society to provide accurate explanation of those events.

← Extremism

Experientialism
Esotericism
Spiritualism
Mysticism

The assertion of experiential and spiritual newness of life, apart from the historical grounding of Jesus' physical resurrection becomes unproven experientialism.

Prayer
Dialectic – Both/And

← Extremism	Verbal	Nonverbal	Extremism →
	Communication	**Communion**	

Verbal

Communication
"when you pray, say ...." (Lk. 11:2)
"Ask, and you will receive" (Jn. 16:24)
"Spirit gave utterance" (Acts 2:4)

audible / inaudible
spoken / unspoken
vocal / non-vocal
oral / silent
public / private
planned / spontaneous

Prayer that uses the con-ventions of grammar and the language the pray-er is familiar with.
Liturgical prayer
- traditions of church

← Extremism

"Saying prayers" can be ritualistic substitute for genuine prayer. - nothing more than spinning a Tibetan prayer-wheel.

The language of prayer must not degenerate into just "words, words, words."

Ritualism
Legalism
Liturgism

Nonverbal

Communion
"having ears to hear what the Spirit is saying..." (Rev. 2,3)
"Spirit intercedes with groanings too deep for words" (Rom. 8:26)
In the Garden - "tells me I am His own"
The heart's true home
- comfort in closeness
- personal connection
- the joy of union
- going with flow of God's grace.
- inner affirmation
- listening obedience
Eucharistic lifestyle of enjoying God's "good grace"
Christ-consciousness
- meditative, contemplative

Extremism →

Internal, subjective praying can become individualized and detached from the community of the saints, the Church.

Mysticism
Asceticism
Quietism
Subjectivism

Prayer

Dialectic – Both/And

103

Extremism	Prewritten	Conversational	Extremism
Some people have become so dependent on prewritten prayers that they have not developed a personal relationship with the Triune God. Meaningless repetition of repeating prescribed prayers can become as much a ritual as the Buddhist "prayer wheel."	Reading of prewritten prayers, perhaps from *Prayer Book or Book of Common Worship.* **Mechanical** - planned and organized recitation and repetition of prewritten prayers can be legitimate means to the end of communing with God, but must not be allowed to be an end in themselves. Meaningless repetition - Matt. 6:7 - "when you pray...do not use meaningless repetition"	Spontaneity of unrehearsed conversational prayer with God - either private or public prayer. **Relational** - prayer is the privilege of the Christian to commune and fellowship in *koinonia* with the Triune God - as "partakers (*koinonoi*) of the divine nature" (II Pt. 1:4), we share in the *koinonia* of the Triune God, and converse with Father, Son and Spirit. Such spontaneous conversation may be in simple words or complex ideas.	Spontaneity of conversation should not be interpreted as unorganized and thoughtless prayer. Conversational prayer can also be repetitious, as some use the same words over and over.

©2014 by James A. Fowler

154

Prayer

Dialectic – Both/And

	Godward	Inward
	Is prayer of any benefit to the God who hears it? - doesn't need anything - knows all in advance	How does prayer benefit the pray-er?
	As personal, relational Being does He take pleasure in relationship with human beings? Undoubtedly!	The mystery of conversing with the Infinite God seems to restructure our thinking to see from His perspective.
	Phil. 4:6 - "in everything by prayer and supplication with thanksgiving, let your requests be made known to God."	There is "something understood" in the depths of our being, even if we are unaware of what God is saying or doing in us.
	Our prayers of thanksgiving, praise, & confession surely bring joy to God's heart.	This may involve awareness of fleshly tendencies and self-denial of such.
		We are listening in the "obedience of faith"

Extremism (Inward side):

It has been suggested that prayer is just a psychological process of auto-suggestion, whereby we hype ourselves into thinking that we know God and what He seeks to do in our lives.

- just wishful thinking that we are connecting with some One beyond ourselves

Extremism (Godward side):

Some have suggested that there is a divine "law of prayer" that inevitably works when the proper procedures are utilized.

Such a mechanical process of prayer reduces relational factor of prayer.

Prayer does not push God's buttons to get Him to act on our behalf.

Prayer

Dialectic – Both/And

Purposeful

Jesus gave His disciples a basic model for purposed prayer.

Matt. 6:9 - "Our Father, who art in heaven..."

Purposed procedures can be beneficial
- time (Quiet Time)
- place (Prayer Chamber) Matt. 6:6 - "inner room"
- written list (Prayer List) of person, situations one wants to remember.

I Tim. 2:1 - "I urge entreaties and prayers...be made on behalf of all men"

Liturgical prayers of the Church
- Prayer Book
- Public worship services
- Prayer partners

Extremism

Proceduralism
Techniquism
- standardizing prayer into pre-set formulas.

Legalism of scheduling a "time of prayer"
- guilt for not spending enough time in prayer.

Liturgism
Ritualism
- unthinking repitition of merely "saying prayers."

Spontaneous

One's heart is caught by surprise in act of prayer.
- driving, reading, working

Lk. 24:32 - "our hearts burned within us"

Times when our inner being senses a closeness and oneness with God.
- transcends intellectual and verbal communication.

- spontaneous pulse of awe, reverence, worship
- Our "spirit-union" (I Cor. 6:17) prompts communion with Triune God.

This can become "prayer without ceasing" (I Thess. 5:17)

This has been called "the prayer of the heart"

Extremism

Spontaneity of prayer must not become an excuse for neglecting purposeful individual prayer and church involvement in prayer.

Individuated spontaneity of prayer has been touted as a form of elitist spirituality.

Christian Security

Dialectic – Both/And

← Extremism

Psychological

Subjectivity
- Inner assurance

I Jn 5:12 - "you may know, and have confidence"

II Tim. 1:12 - "I know … and am convinced"

Rom. 8:16 - Spirit bears witness with my spirit"

Procedural basis:
- secure that I have engaged in the right actions:
  - walked the aisle
  - repeated the creed
  - signed church covenant

Epistemological basis:
- secure that I have believed and assented to the right/correct tenets of Christian faith.

Christological

Objectivity
- Security of relationship based beyond oneself in the Divine Person of Jesus Christ.
- based on the dynamic eternality and permanence of the very Being of the Triune God.

Faithfulness of God in Christ by the Spirit
- Jn. 6:37 - "not cast out"
- Jn. 10:38 - "no one can snatch them out…"
- Heb. 13:5 - "I will never desert you or forsake you"
- I Cor. 1:8 - "confirm you to the end"
- I Pt. 1:5 - "protected by the power of God"

Extremism →

Mental and emotional criteria for awareness of secure relationship:
- "burning bosom"
- "inner tickle"
- "know that I know"
- "It's in my pocket and it can't get out"
- "I believe in 'once saved, always saved'"

Personal uncertainty of relationship with God.

Denial that subjective feelings have anything to do with relationship with Christ.

Assertion that personal faithfulness has nothing to do with relationship with Christ.

107

Worship

Dialectic – Both/And

Extremism	Public	Private	Extremism
Ritualism Liturgism -specified procedures performed by priests. - Clericalism - Programmed proceduralism Worship occurs only at a specific time and place. - church building - 11 am Sunday morning. Collective experience of entertainment or excitement. - Experientialism - "Happy, clappy" worship services	Liturgical worship - in accord with the church calendar - in accord with the specified prayer book Regular and periodic scheduling of assembly for the worship of the saints. Collective, planned program of worship. Jesus Christ is our High Priest and minister in the sanctuary -Heb.8:1,2;9:11 Risen and living Lord Jesus is the subject and the object of Christian worship. Objective: "to the praise of the glory of His grace" (Eph. 1:6)	Lifestyle worship - constant and spontaneous expression of worship by Christian individuals. - unique expression in individual Christians Expresses the worth-ship of the divine Being and character in the behavior of a Christian person. Every act of the Christian life is to be an act of worship. - actuated by God's grace - faithful receptivity of God's activity. Christian worship must be Christ in action in us. "Worship Him in Spirit and in truth" (Jn. 4:24)	Asceticism Monasticism Quietism Individualism - "do it yourself" worship. Anthropocentric worship wherein the "blessing" of the worshipper is the objective. Behaviorism - quality of worship determined by our outcomes.

©2014 by James A. Fowler

158

Sharing Christ

Dialectic – Both/And

Extremism	Teaching	Testimony	Extremism
Believing that the Christian faith is primarily an epistemological "belief-system," the Church has viewed itself as an educational institution, requiring catechismal instruction in the creedal data. Content of Christian doctrine without experience of the living Jesus is but sterile information.	Instructing others about the "facts" of the history and meaning of the life of Jesus Christ. The didactic teaching of the Church has historically been the recitation of the collectively accepted theological doctrine and dogma as expressed in the creeds. The primary source of the Church's teaching has been the Biblical record of "revealed truth." This instruction has often been theoretical data.	Sharing how God has worked the life of Jesus into one's life. - experiential - personal Allowing the indwelling life of Jesus to overflow into the lives of others. Must allow every person who shares, testifies, witnesses of Jesus to proclaim what he/she has come to know experientially and subjectively. Soren Kierkegaard - "Truth is subjectivity."	Subjectivism Experientialism Some, like Rudolph Bultmann, have indicated that the historical events of Christianity and the creedal statements of Christian faith are secondary (even irrelevant), for one's personal experience is the only "truth" that is important.

Ministry

Dialectic – Both/And

← Extremism (Particular)	Particular	Inclusive	Extremism → (Inclusive)
Ecclesiasticism Professionalism - attempting to operate the Church like an organization with a "business model." Pride of position and power.	Christian ministry in the context of the Church requires ministerial leadership. "Jesus appointed twelve" (Mk. 3:14,16) "Lord appointed seventy others" (Lk. 10:1) "appointed elders in every church" (Acts 14:23) "I was appointed preacher, teacher, ..." (II Tim 1:11) "fulfill your ministry" (II Tim. 4:5) Leaders need to be theologically educated, and vocationally trained. "Ministry of the word" (Acts 6:4)	Christian ministry in the context of the Church involves participation of every believer. Priesthood of all believers - (I Peter 2:5,9) Ministry of all believers - (Eph. 4:12 - "equipping of the saints for the work of ministry") "God appointed in the church, apostles, prophets, teachers, ..." (I Cor. 12:28) Every Christian has been spiritually gifted to function in the church in the ministry of Jesus. Ministry is the overflow of the life of Jesus to others. "Serve one another" (Gal. 5:13)	The involvement of all Christians without the oversight of trained Christian leaders can result in - "zeal without knowledge" (Rom. 10:2) - spiritual pride of assuming positions of control. Individualism Temperamentalism

©2014 by James A. Fowler

Pastor

Dialectic – Both/And

Extremism

Contemporary pastoral position has often become
- ecclesiastical office
- professional career
- vocational aspiration

Clericalism and distinct clergy/laity separation. Required theological and administrative training, often with little or no emphasis on spiritual maturity.

Position in Church

As the church developed organizationally into a hierarchical institution, pastoral position became prominant in local church
- identified as parson, preacher, padre, priest, minister, reverend, clergy

Questions of:
- pastoral responsibility? preach, counsel, administrate, worship leader
- pastoral accountability? local church (employee?) denomination, God
- pastoral authority?

Is pastor authority over local church?

I Pet. 5:3 - "not lording it over those allotted to your charge ...."

Spiritual Giftedness

The word "pastor" in the New Testament is Greek word for "shepherd" (*poimen*)

Eph. 4:11 - "God gave some as pastors and teachers"

God gifts some individuals with spiritual wisdom and ability to shepherd the flock of God's people, the Church.

A pastor is but an under-shepherd of the "Great Shepherd," Jesus Christ (cf. Heb. 13:20)

I Pet. 2:25 - "Shepherd and Guardian of our souls"

Jn. 10:2-16-Good Shepherd

Responsibility to "equip the saints" (Eph. 4:12) and "care for saints" (Acts 20)

Extremism

Some have claimed a self-determined spiritual giftedness of pastoring.

-determination of such giftedness should be made in the collective of the church.

Claims to pastoral giftedness without ancillary of pastoral training has led to much confusion and misrepresentation.

Healing

Dialectic – Both/And

Extremism	Physical	Whole Person	Extremism
Mistaken concepts of bodily healing; "God does not intend for anyone to die physically". "Healing is in the atonement," and all physical ailments are promised to be healed if one exercises faith in Christ's redemptive death." Isa. 53:5 - "by His stripes we are healed" (I Pet. 2:24; Matt 8:17) Abuses of "faith-healing"	God created our physical bodies and can certainly heal the ailments of the human body if He so wills Supernatural physical healing was a sign that God was working in Jesus and His followers. Matt. 9:35 - "Jesus healing every kind of disease ... sickness" God is a healing and restoring God, and continues to heal in every age. - "gifts of healing" (I Cor. 12:9,28,30) Such divine healing does not preclude natural medical processes of healing. Mk. 2:7 - "the sick have need of a physician."	Christians expect the eventual total, eternal well-being of the entire person in the heavenly realm. Rev. 21:4 - "He will wipe away every tear from their eyes; and there will no longer be any death; there will no longer be any mourning, or crying, or pain..." In this sense it can be said that physical death can be viewed as the ultimate healing of an individual. - avoidance of physical death is not a Christian aspiration. Phil. 1:23 - "desire to depart and be with Christ, for that is far better"	Some Christians believe that the supernatural sign gifts were only for the apostolic period, and that after the New Testament period supernatural physical healing is not to be expected. Some have argued that the whole person is healed in regeneration, and all physical ailments are just an illusion.

©2014 by James A. Fowler

Church History

Dialectic – Both/And

Extremism →

→ **Perversion**

Perfection ←

← **Extremism**

Perfection

The Christian Church is not essentially and intrinsically perfect in character, as only God is.

The Church has, however, evidenced perfection in the Greek sense of *teleiosis*, i.e. functioning in accord with the end and objective for which it was instituted by God.

Such "perfection" is evidenced when the "Body of Christ," the Church allows for the individual and collective expression of the life and character of the living Lord Jesus.

Perversion

The history of the Christian Church reveals that the Church has often failed to function as intended by God, and has often misrepresented Christ in sinful perversion and corruption.

Ecclesiastical perversions include, but not limited to:
- inquisitions, crusades
- witch hunts
- financial extortion
- indulgences
- pastoral immorality
- pedophilia
- excommunication abuse
- papal power-plays
- child/elder abuse

(left Extremism)

The Church has often been elevated by the faithful to a place of being beyond criticism.

Basing their opinions on I Sam. 26:9-23, church leaders have often avoided critique for being "the Lord's anointed."

(right Extremism)

Ecclesiastical perversion often goes unchecked when a policy of "separation of church and state" forestalls legal accountability for otherwise illegal activities.

Also when ecclesiastical authorities protect their own and do not hold them accountable for moral turpitude.

The Christian and the the World

Dialectic – Both/And

Extremism	In the world	Not of the world	Extremism
Accomodationism Adaptationism Capitulation Compromise Acquiesence Appeasement Synthesize Submergionism	Jn. 17:11 - "they themselves are in the world"	Jn. 17:14 - "they (disciples of Jesus) are not of the world, even as I am not of the world.	Escapism Separationism Withdrawal Detachment Asceticism Monasticism Disengagement Uninvolved Avoidance
	Jn. 17:18 - "As You sent Me into the world, I also have sent them into the world.	Jn. 17:16 - They are not of the world, even as I am not of the world.	
	Jn. 17:17 - "I do not ask You to take them out of the world, but to keep them from the evil one. "	Jn. 18:36 - "my kingdom is not of this world"	
Adopting the methods and techniques of the world. Attempts to change, reform, improve or "save the world." Reconstructionism	Matt. 5:13 - "you are the salt of the earth" Matt. 5:14 - "you are the light of the world" Matt. 13:33 - "the kingdom of heaven is like leaven" (cf. Lk. 13:21) Acts 1:8 - "you shall be My witnesses to the remotest part of the earth"	II Cor. 6:14 - "Do not be bound together with unbelievers;..." II Cor. 6:17 - "come out from their midst and be separate" I Pet. 2:11 - "strangers and aliens" Heb. 11:13 - "citizens of heaven" *Ecclesia* - "called out"	Ghetto mentality Bombshelter mentality Christian sub-culture Become "Holy Huddle" Repudiation of the world Make war with the world

Interactive

Both/And Dialectics

dealing with

Social Issues

Human Interactions/Sociology

Dialectic – Both/And

← Extremism	Conflict	Peace	Extremism →
Crusaderism war-mongers	Primary theory of secular sociology	Amicable fellowship Loving community	Utopianism
"might makes right" "may the best one win" "In it to win it!"	- disagreement, animosity, opposition, discord, contention, rivalry, competition, rancor, fight	- agreement, harmony, conciliation, accord, civility, mutuality	Idealism of "heaven on earth"
	Opposing opinions: nationality, race, religion, gender, age, ideology, preferences.	Matt. 5:9 - "blessed are the peacemakers"	Ambivalence "who gives a damn?"
Fight to the death - decimation of enemy.	Fallen world system "my way" - selfishness	Jn. 20:19 - "Peace be with you."	Peaceful coexistence despite beliefs or conduct
	Judg. 17:6 - "Every man did what was right in his own eyes"	Rom. 12:18 - be at peace with all men	Pluralism - believe what you will; peace at any cost
Fundamentalism - tends to fight over correct belief system	"In this world you will have tribulation" (Jn 16:33)	Rodney King - "why can't we all get along"	
		Agree to disagree	
		NOT merely absence of conflict	

Institutions

Dialectic – Both/And

Divine

← Extremism

God-ordained institutions:
- Human volition

  Gen. 2:7-17 - God Self-limited Himself to create response-able choosing derivative creatures.

- Marriage

  Gen. 2:18-25 - God instituted the relational union of one man and one woman in marriage.

- Government

  Rom. 13:1-7 - "no governing authority except from God." to provide order, rule, control...

- Church - *ecclesia*

  Matt. 16:18 - "I will build My church."
  Jesus is Head of Church cf. Eph. 1:22,23; Col. 1:18

Extremism (Divine):

Humanism
Absolutism
Fundamentalism

Idealism
Proceduralism
Techniquism

Governmental totalitarianism
- abuse of power

Ecclesiastical imposition

Human

← Extremism

Human institutions and organizations necessary for implementing form & structure of divine institutions.

Such institutions may be:
- ideological
- legal
- social
- cultural
- national
- community, public
- political
- moral
- economic
- educational
- athletic
- religious
- business
- benevolent
- medical

Extremism (Human):

Institutionalism
Structuralism
Formalism
Authoritarianism
Humanism

Making human institutions sacrosanct.
- deifying one's ideology, political persuasions, nationalism, patriotism, religionism.

Government

Dialectic – Both/And

Extremism → Individualism	Personal Privacy Rights	National Security	Extremism → Collectivism
Individualism - "every man for himself" - "stand up for your rights"	Uniqueness of our government with defined and amplified "Bill of Rights," expressing individual rights and freedoms. right to personal safety and protection	Individuals must recognize they are part of a greater whole, and that nation is responsible for the safety and protection of all.	Collectivism The safety of the whole is more important than the rights of individuals.
"our personal rights are what constitute and define our nation"	right to freedom of speech and press within context. right to freedom of religion and worship practice right to privacy of person (modesty) and personal information.	When the safety and preservation of the nation is at jeopardy, individual rights and liberties may have to be restricted or sacrificed to preserve existence and security of nation.	"Only the *idiots* would 'save their own butts,' while watching the national ship sink."
"Those who would give up essential liberty to purchase a temporary safety deserve neither liberty nor safety." - Ben Franklin	right to earn money and spend as desired. right to protect property right to protect reputation against defamation right to pursuit of personal happiness	Where will the individual rights and freedoms be if there is no nation to guarantee those rights? Democratic government must eschew despotism.	"Those who would give up national security for the exercise of personal rights, deserve neither security or liberty."

Politics – Social Governance

Dialectic – Both/And

	Preservation	Progression	
Extremism			Extremism

Preservation	Progression
Need to preserve the heritage of our cultural values and traditions.	Need to look ahead to see how we can progress and improve and advance.
Need to respect and preserve what our forefathers have constructed.	Need to change, move on, make progress to stay at the forefront.
Past orientation - realization of what is most important and what is worth keeping.	Future orientation - onward and upward to innovation and advancement
Conservative traditions, conformity of common values	Liberal non-conformity - "time to try something new and different"
Institutional thinking - "we're in this together"	Individuated thinking - personal potential

Preservation extremes	Progression extremes
Conservatism	Liberalism
Preservationism	Progressivism
Traditionalism	Utilitarianism
Historicism	Pluralism
Absolutism	Multi-culturalism
Moralism	Relativism
	Pragmatism
Obstructionism	Materialism
- stuck in the rut of the past.	Activism
- "we've never done it that way before!"	Social deconstructivism
-retrograde mind-set	Anti-institutional
	Cynicism
Status-quo stagnation	Utopianism - keep getting better and better.
Republican party	Democratic party

Social Governance

Dialectic – Both/And

Extremism (Individual Freedom)	Individual Freedom	Social Order	Extremism (Social Order)
Individualism	Individual human beings have an intrinsic right for freedom to pursue their own happiness and objectives.	Societal laws are required to maintain order and safety for all in the social unit.	Socialism
Selfism			Authoritarianism Despotism
Persons become a "law unto themselves" - "did what was right in their own eyes" (Deut. 12:8)	Personal freedom to seek meaning and purpose require personal character and responsibility.	Social participation involves social responsibilities, duties, and contribution to the welfare of the whole.	Governmentalism
	American Constitutional "Bill of rights"	I Pet. 2:13 - "submit to human institutions"	Governmental intrustion - restriction of human rights
Libertinism Libertarianism Anarchism	I Pet. 2:16 - "act as free men"	Heb. 13:14 - "obey your leaders and submit"	Oppressive laws
Those not interested in the whole - Gk. *idiotes*			

> "Society cannot exist unless a controlling power upon will and appetite be placed somewhere, and the less of it there is within, the more there will be without." - Edward Burke

Immigration

Dialectic – Both/And

← Extremism →

Government Protection of Citizenry

Government has right of national sovereignty and obligation to protect its borders and citizenry.

Government has jurisdiction to establish bases of citizenship,

- responsibility to protect resources of country,

- right to mandate all immigrants obey all laws.

- must protect citizens from accommodation to customs of foreigners (Deut. 28:43,44)

Government is a minister of God for us for good, and for the avenging of evil" (Romans 13:4)

Human Concern for Asylum-seekers

Responsible, God-fearing citizens have obligation to protect displaced, asylum-seekers, refugees, and immigrants.

Lev. 19:34 - "The stranger who resides with you shall be to you as the native among you, and you shall love him as yourself"

Deut. 10:18 - "show love for the alien by giving him food and clothing."

Matt. 25:40 - "to the extent that you did it to the least of these you did it to Me"

Heb. 13:2 - "do not neglect to show hospitality to strangers..."

Extremism (left)

Nationalism
Protectionism
Isolationism
Utopianism
Self-preservation
Excuses:
- social burden
- economic threat
- security threat
Fear-based reactions
- ambivalence,
- "full; no vacancy; go home"
- dehumanization of "others," the "outsiders"
- no tolerance for "illegals"

Extremism (right)

Humanitarianism
- "human rights"
Sentimentalism
- "bleeding heart" sym/empathy
- presented as selfless altruism
- based on secularistic pluralism and multi-culturalism.
Advocacy of "open borders" and amnesty for all.
Premise of abject victim-objects is terrible victimization and dehumanization.

©2014 by James A. Fowler

Citizenship and War

Dialectic – Both/And

← Extremism

← Extremism

Earthly Nation	Spiritual Kingdom
Rom. 13:1 - "Let every person be in subjection to the governing authorities" I Pet. 2:13 - "Submit yourselves to every human institution."	Phil. 3:20 - "our citizenship is in heaven." Matt. 5:9 - "blessed are the peacemakers" Matt. 26:52 - "those who take up the sword shall perish by the sword."
Right of nation to protect itself and citizens - armed defense - retributive justice - preserve human rights	Jn. 18:36 - "If My kingdom was of this world, then My servants would fight" Aversion & resistance to - world's power-struggles - conflict and war
Responsibility of citizens to obey government, but not unreservedly or slavishly.	Right of individual Christian to act on basis of conviction (Rom. 14:5) and conscience (Heb. 13:18; I Pet. 2:19)
Concept of "just war" - Augustine and Aquinas	

Nationalism
Patriotism
"our country, right or wrong"

Militarism
- aggression
- invasion
- occupation
- domination
- Crusades
- *jihad*

Pacifism
Idealism

Passivism
- avoidance
- non-involvement

Isolationism
Escapism

Self-preservation
Cowardice

Conflict and War

Dialectic – Both/And

Confrontational	Non-confrontational
Extremism	**Extremism**
Warrior God -Exod. 15:3-Lord is warrior -Ps. 24:8 - "Lord strong in battle"	• Messiah - God's deliverer - Isa. 9:6 - "Prince of Peace" - Micah 4:3-5 - "beat swords into plowshares"
Time for war - Eccl. 3:8 - "a time for war" - Joel 3:9 - "prepare a war; plowshares into swords"	• Peacemakers - Matt. 5:9-11 - "blessed are the peacemakers"
Offensive war - "Numb. 31:7 - "they made war, as Lord commanded	• New covenant love - Matt. 5:44 "love enemies"
Defensive war - II Kgs 20:6 "I will defend this city, for My sake"	• Non-resistance - Matt. 5:39 - "do not resist him who is evil"
Do justice - Ps. 82:1-4 - "do just to the afflicted; deliver from the wicked"	• Non-retaliatory - Rom. 12:17-19 - "Never pay back evil for evil"
Governmental authority - I Pt 2:13-17 - "governors sent by God to punish...	• Non-hostile - Matt. 5:21 - "everyone who is angry is guilty"
	• Positive action - Rom. 12:20 - "if enemy is hungry, feed him....

Extremism

War-mongers
- Ps. 68:30 - those who delight in war

Militarism
Nationalism
Patriotism

Constantine
"By this sign, conquer"

Crusades
- "God is on our side"
- "Holy war" against infidels

Power and force are the only solution

Extremism

Passivism
- acquiesence

Non-involvement
- Isolationism

Idealism
- "visualize peace, eliminate hate"
- "make love, not war"
- essential good of mankind will avoid war

Ideological
Legalism
"All war is wrong, immoral, unjust"

Social Progress

Dialectic – Both/And

Extremism	Institutional	Individual	Extremism
Socialism Communalism Statism Egalitarianism Wealth redistribution Entitlement - "I have a right to have what you have."	Collective activity of social institutions to be concerned for the whole.	Individual person freedom and incentive to "be all I can be."	Individualism - narcissism - selfishness - "each person must do his best"
	Church, government, benevolence agencies.	Human responsibility for moral propriety.	
	Preserve equal rights - concern for less-fortunate, poor, disadvantaged, hungry, handicapped, - social action, reform, stand against injustice via institutional improvement	Promote equal opportunity - personal success, prosperity, economic efficiency, innovation - internal change of spiritual character, respect for others, self-sacrifice and personal improvement	Capitalism Plutocracy Aversion to taxation
Big government social programs	Promotes giving, sharing, providing for others	Promotes acquisition	Conservatism - "We've never done it that way before."
"Bleeding heart" altruism	Takes into account basic collective concern for fairness and equity.	Selfish aspirations can be spiritually exchanged for loving character of Christ.	Materialism

Human Existence - Life/Death

Dialectic – Both/And

Extremism ← ... → Extremism

"Right to Life" (Extremism)	Divine Determination	Human Determination	"Right to Choose" / Humanism (Extremism)
"Right to Life" movement opposes abortion and euthanasia on the grounds that human determination should not override Divine determination.	Divine determination of life and death	Human self-determination of life and death.	"Right to Choose" movement often denies any legitimacy to divine determination in the realm of physical life or death.
Divine Determinism - "dignity of human life" can become a way of deifing human life.	Life and death are determined by and derived from spiritual source. - "time to be born, time to die" - Eccl. 3:2 - Heb. 2:14 - "one having the power of death" - Job 33:4 - "the Almighty gives me life" - Jn 5:21 - "Father gives life … Son gives life" - Jn 6:63 - "Spirit gives life"	Human beings designed to live and die by the consequences of their choices. - freedom of choice - choosing creatures	Humanism - deification of human volition and the choice to make ultimate determinations of life and death.
	Divine determination of the dignity of human life and death.	Human beings can, and do, make choices to allow for • physical life or death - abortion - euthanasia - suicide, murder • spiritual life or death - rejection of life offer - regeneration unto life in Christ Jesus - apostasy	

Determinations of Life and Death

Dialectic – Both/And

Extremism →	Dignity of Life	Quality of Life	← Extremism
Conservatism	Intrinsic worth, value, sanctity of human life. - determined by God's order and structure. - mankind created as highest order of life.	Human choices difficult in real-world situations. - determined by man's evaluation of acceptability - God created humans as choosing creatures.	Liberalism
Ideological Absolutism - God has determined absolutes - Civil laws legislate such - Vitalism – "right to life" preserved with no "right to choose quality."	Distinct biological, ideological polarity between physical life and death.	Specrum of acceptability between "life lived to the fullest" - "mere existence"	Ideological Relativism - Individual right to determination of quality of life and death. - Basic "right to death" by self-chosen means. - No "right to kill"
	Intrinsic "right to life" inherent in created order.	Created "right to choose" in human responsibility.	
Inordinate respect for human life may become bio-idolatry.	Society must respect as inviolable the individual's right to live.	Individual right to choose acceptable quality of life, or designate others to do so. - "Living Will" with "durable power of attorney/ health proxy"	Tolerance of choices may become deification of reason.
Fearful of medical technology manipulating life.	Medical field honors dignity of life. - Hippocratic oath		Fearful of Theocratic tyranny.

Human Reasoning

Dialectic – Both/And

Deductive	Inductive
Top-down logic - *a priori* - prior determination - archetypal origin and source	Bottom-up logic - *a posteriori* - reasoning back to source - ectypal observation of the type
Projection of ideas - noumenal - conceptual - suppositional - ideological categories	Evaluation of things - phenomenal - perceptual - evidentiary - observed manifestations
Being *a se* - in itself - objective reality is inferred as self-evident and self-existent	Doing - examination - subjective involvement of the do-er analyzing observed data
Abstract and intangible generalization - "In the beginning God.."	Concrete and tangible particularization - Arguments for God's existence

Extremism (Deductive side):
- Platonism
- Projectionism
- Idealism
  - the "really real" is intangible and cannot be seen"
- Supernaturalism
- Metaphysical
- Creationism
- Universal
- Objectivism
- Augustinianism

Extremism (Inductive side):
- Aristotelianism
- Empiricism
- Realism
  - the "really real" is what you see and touch"
- Naturalism
- Physical
- Scientism
- Cosmological
- Subjectivism
- Thomism

Rationality

Dialectic – Both/And

Extremism	Human Logic	TheoLogic	Extremism
Rationalism Cognitivism Intellectualism Naturalism Empiricism Pseudo-absolutes	Finite human reasoning - noumenal; *nous*=mind - mental consideration - propositional truths - transferrable knowledge Enlightenment elevated empirical knowledge of physical world.	Infinite divine wisdom is made known by revelation - "knowing" beyond human explication - open-ended mystery - apophatic theology - faith supersedes reason	Fideism Mysticism Spiritualism Irrationalism Anti-intellectual-ism
Intellectual pride - I Cor 8:1 - "know-ledge makes arrogant"	I Cor. 3:19 - "wisdom of this world is foolishness" I Cor. 1:21 - "wisdom of world does not know God" I Cor. 2:14 - things of God are foolishness" I Cor. 2:14 - "does not understand spiritual things"	I Co. 1:21 - "wisdom of God I Cor 2:7 - "Gods wisdom in a mystery" Isa. 55:8,9 - "My thoughts are not your thoughts..." I Cor. 2:13 - "taught by Spirit, combining spiritual thoughts with spiritual words"	*Aporia* - doesn't compute - incomprehen-sible - perplexity - befuddlement
"It can't be true if it doesn't make sense to me" - Human mind is the final arbiter of truth	"Learned ignorance" - Nicolas of Cusa Either/or dichotomies - "law of non-contradiction - "excluded middle?	Spiritual discernment "Coincidence of opposites" - Nicolas of Cusa Both/and dialectics - cf. Kierkegaard	"Don't try to understand; just trust God"

Prophecy
Dialectic – Both/And

Extremism (Foretell)	Foretell	Forthtell	Extremism (Forthtell)
Futurism - human beings preoccupied with space/time calculations.	Gk. *prophetes* - to speak before in terms of time.	Gk. *prophetes* - to speak before personal hearers.	Gnosticism - human beings preoccupied with wanting to know.
- perverse desire of fallen mankind to know what will come - often precludes faith. - often results in wild speculations	Prediction	Proclamation	Often becomes an informational priority with content of teaching, rather than personal relational priority of hearing what God desires to speak to our hearts.
	God knows the end from the beginning, but His primary intent is not the implementation of a prescribed agenda in time.	The relational Triune God is concerned about having relationality with humans, by speaking into their hearts.	
Proceduralism - attempting to get God and His ways figured out. - want Divine Plan and agenda to self-determine.	Old Covenant prophecy (cf. II Peter 1:21) often had double entendre: - short term & long term - Israel and Messiah	New covenant obedience, *hupakouo*, is "to listen under" His speaking.	
	New covenant "gift of prophecy" - cf. Rom. 12:6; I Cor. 12:10; 13:2,8; 14:1,6	Kerygma - to proclaim or herald in Christocentric evangelistic preaching Didache - to teach or train via Christocentric exposition and catechesis.	

Apocalypse
Dialectic – Both/And

Cryptic Vision

The symbolic imagery employed in the Apocalypse is consistent with that of apocalyptic literature from post-exilic Judaic history.

- cryptic imagery from mythological and cosmological traditions were used to illustrate and reveal hidden realities.

Variety of hermeneutic methods utilized to interpret these cryptic images throughout Christian history of thought.

- preterist (past)
- historicist
- futurist
- symbolist (triumphalist)

Extremism

Some have judged the imagery of the revelation to be so cryptic as to be incapable of interpretation.

Some preoccupied with identifying the meaning of the images.

- preterists (Roman emperors)
- historicists (Roman church or world leaders)
- futurists (speculate on future nations or leader)

Christus Victor

Important to approach the Apocalypse from a Christ-centered perepective.

- It is the revelation or unveiling of the living Lord Jesus Christ (1:1)

Conflict is the setting of the Apocalypse. There is a war going on!

There is no doubt that the victor of the conflict is Jesus Christ.

- Gustaf Aulén wrote *Christus Victor* in 1931.

Diverse identification of adversary in apocalypse:
- cf. Roman emperors, Roman church, religion...

Extremism

Some have over-generalized and "spiritualized" the cryptic images in resigned obscurantism:
- "It doesn't matter what the symbols mean; we know who wins in the end!"

Triumphalism
- Some so confident of Christ's ultimate victory they become passive & apathetic.

Christian Dialectics

Dialectic – Both/And

Objective	Subjective
External - outside of how we think, feel and choose.	Internal - inside of our spiritual and psychic being
Truth-tenets should be accurately based on legitimate data regardless of our acceptance or belief in such.	It is important that our mental assent, emotional feelings, and volitional acceptance align with the objective data.
Doctrinal Theological Philosophical	Practical - practicum Experiential Behavioral
Some personalities are more objective-oriented.	Some personalities are more subjective-oriented.

Extremism (left) · Extremism (right)

Objective extreme:

Doctrinalism
Evangelicalism
Fundamentalism

Those who conceive of Christianity as a belief-system, tend to focus on the content of information rather than on the transformation of personal lives.

Believe-right religion.

Subjective extreme:

Subjectivism
Experientialism
Behaviorism

Those who emphasize the practicality of motivations, attitudes and behavior, often regard doctrinal and theological matters to be irrelevant and extraneous.

Do-right religion.

God calls some teachers to emphasize one leg or one rail of a dialectic more than the other. Primary emphasis does not necessarily mean that a dialectic balance is not being maintained. And some listeners prefer to hear instruction emphasizing one side or the other.

©2014 by James A. Fowler

Christian Understanding

Dialectic – Both/And

Dialectics	Single Focus
"The Dialectic Formatting of Christian Thought and Practice."	The "single-eye" of Faith, focused on relationality with the living Lord Jesus. (cf. Matt. 6:22; Lk. 11:32)
"Every coin has two sides" - Every issue in human and Christian thought has more than one perspective.	*Sola Christos* was the Reformation motto.
II Pet. 3:18 - "*both* now *and* to the day of eternity" - Already / Not yet	Lk. 10:42 - "one thing is necessary" (faith that listens to Jesus)
Expanded horizons of thought allow for greater understanding and communicative interaction in the Christian community.	The singularity of Jesus Christ and the singularity of the Christian's focused participation in Christ as their life.

↑ Extremism

Fideism
- one shouldn't attempt to use their mind to see the broader perspective of Christian thinking.
- Just faith it!

Subjectivism

"dialectics is a form of relativism"

"A double-minded man is unstable in all his ways" (James 1:8)

↓ Extremism

Dialecticism
- everything can be understood when put into a chart showing the contrasting perspectives of every category.

"An individual who cannot see both sides of an issue is destined to extremism."

Objectivism

Conclusion

CONCLUSION

The foregoing dialectic charts are but a few of the ever-growing, seemingly never-ending development of *both/and* dialectic charts that keep my mind going back and forth day after day. They keep waking me up early in the morning, and keep my wife shaking her head in disbelief at my bobble-head brain!

The forgoing sequence of charts is a formatting for Christian thought that attempts to keep a balanced perspective of various themes, while avoiding the extremes that have so often become *either/or* conflicts that have long dominated Christian thinking and interaction. This study could be developed into a unique form of balanced systematic theology, if someone had the time and inclination to flesh out these skeletal charts (others of their own making) with elaborated explanation and commentary.

In the midst of this study on "the dialectic formatting of Christian thought," you may have discovered that there were categories where you have tended to take a "one-sided perspective" that may have failed to take into consideration both sides of God's revealed truths. It is sometimes difficult for our minds and ego-pride to allow for a readjustment of our thinking, to recognize and admit that there may be areas where we have slid off into an "....ism" ditch, rather than taking into account the "full counsel of God" (Acts 20:27 – KJB). It is always healthy to expand our horizons, and to become more accepting and appreciative of other perspectives and the people who hold those opinions. Part of the value of this study is that it can stretch our thinking, and cause us to realize that many of these subjects are broader than we may have realized.

Perhaps a caution is also in order concerning these dialectic charts. As we have shared these dialectic charts, one after another in category after category, it may appear that this creates clean, clear-cut diagrams, providing precise explanations of the contrasts of human and Christian thought, and the corresponding extremes of over-emphasis.

It is only fair that I caution you to beware. Dialectics can be a messy business! There are some slippery slopes, some melding crossovers that can cause your brain to get fuzzy and go mushy! One form of dialectic can be embedded inside of another dialectic. One side of a dialectic can be subdivided into numerous other dialectics. It is quite understandable why some people mistakenly regard dialectic thought as a form of "relativism" that refuses to construct any absolutes. And they even quote James' statement, "A double-minded man is unstable in all his ways" (James 1:8). In dialectic theological thinking there is no doubt that the definitiveness and precision that theologians like to think they have figured out and can then assert as the "truth" is diminished; and Christian thinkers consequently have to be more honest about the finitude of their reasoning processes.

We certainly do not want to give the impression that by the use of these charts, or that by the dialectic thinking process one can get everything "figured out," "cut-and-dried," "nailed down," or that this dialectic formatting should necessarily become a required exercise in the analysis and systematization of human or Christian belief. We must beware that such a study as this might lead to an undue elevation or even a *deification* of the dialectic process. Yes, we must even give a warning against excessive dialecticizing!!

Perhaps this study of dialectics has stretched the parameters of your belief-system, provided there is enough elasticity and flexibility in your thinking, and your mind is not set in concrete. The reader may discover they have to do a re-think of some tenets they thought were valid. On the other hand, if this study fails to lead people into a deeper trusting faith in a personal relationship with the risen and living Lord Jesus, then it could conceivably be a detriment to some people's faith. Feel free to question and reject this formatting tool of dialectics.

There is no correct way to construct these diagrams of dialectic. Everyone will construct them differently. I have drawn hundreds of charts, and many of them incorporate elements of other charts. This is just a formatting procedure for "seeing two sides" of various themes. What we have proposed is just a stereoscopic lens for looking at various Christian categories.

I have found that the dialectic formatting of Christian thought and practice gives me a sense of mental balance and helps me to avoid the extremes in the avoidance of fundamentalism, Gnosticism, fideism and several thousand other man-made ...isms of human formulation. For over two decades now, the dialectic perspective has become the infrastructure of my theological thinking. But, on the other hand, neither do I want to fall into an extremist ditch of dialecticism as a procedural necessity of Christian thinking.

It is possible, as you can see in the final dialectic chart (#130), to place the concept of "dialectic" within a dialectic diagram. The objective process of the dialectic formatting of Christian thought and practice is juxtaposed with the subjective process of viewing God and His ways with the "single eye" of faith. Aberrant extremisms exist when either approach is emphasized to the denial, diminishment, or neglect of the other. It is possible to so focus on objective dialectic formatting to the neglect of a personal faith-focus, that one falls into the ditch of dialecticism. On the other hand, some have so emphasized the subjective focus of faith that they have fallen into the ditch of fideism. Only when the objective and subjective elements of Christian faith are maintained in balanced equilibrium do we present the gospel honestly and with integrity.

By all means we want to avoid disparaging the "single eye" focus of faith on the singularity of the Savior, Jesus Christ, that allows individuals to participate personally and subjectively in Christ by receptivity in the divine life, love and reality of God in Christ by the Spirit. That is where all our ponderings should lead us, to a deep and intimate personal relationship with the living Lord Jesus Christ.

Addendum

Dichotomous Polarities
Either / Or

God	Satan
God	Humanity
Creator	Creature
Independent	Dependent
Good	Evil
Spirit of truth	Spirit of error
Holiness	Sin
Righteousness	Iniquity
Christ	Adam
Christian	Natural man
Grace	Performance
Spirit	Flesh
Heaven	Hell

NOT Dialectics – i.e. Both / And
NOT Dualisms – like Yin / Yang

Addendum A

Terminology

Binary – "twofold" – base-two digital computing

Polarity – Divergent poles of contrasting ideas or actions; bipolar

Paradox – two idea or statements that "appear alongside" of one another and appear to be contradictory or incongruous.

Antinomy – diverse concepts that are "against the law of reason;" they are mutually incompatible or involve an irresolvable contradiction.

Dichotomy – "cut in two" – dissection or bifurcation into two Parts

Dualism – demarcation of two opposites. Classical definition of two mutually exclusive and absolute equal forces in perpetual stalemate or stand-off

Dialectic – (*dia*=through; *lecto*=talk) "To speak or converse through" various contrasting issues or ideas. Divergent history:

Socrates – dialogue, discussion and cross-examination of ideas
Plato – "theory of ideas" allowing for mutual consensus
Aristotle – formal logic of syllogistic argumentation
Abelard – *Sic et Non* (So & No); pseudo and anti dialecticians
Nicolas of Cusa – *"coincidentia oppositorum"* – contrasting
    thoughts must be viewed from God's perspective.
Hegel – triadic integration of thesis, antithesis into synthesis
Marx – "dialectical materialism" – progressively liberate
    oppressed peoples to produce materialistic egalitarianism.
Kierkegaard – experiential (existential) dialectic. "Absolute
    Paradox" of the incarnation and crucifixion of Jesus Christ.
Jean-Paul Sartre – secular existentialist dialectic philosophy.
Karl Barth – "Dialectic Theology" – knowability of God through
    His Self-revelation in Jesus Christ.
Jacques Ellul – dialectic of complementarity and reciprocity

Dialectic Diversity

Hegel's Synthetic Reductionism

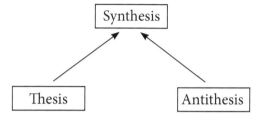

Kierkegaard's Inverted Existentialism

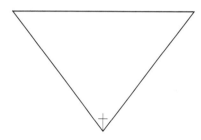

Interactive Both/And Dialectics

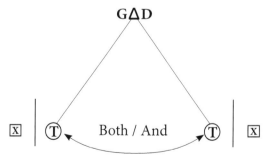

Hegel's
Synthetic Reductionism

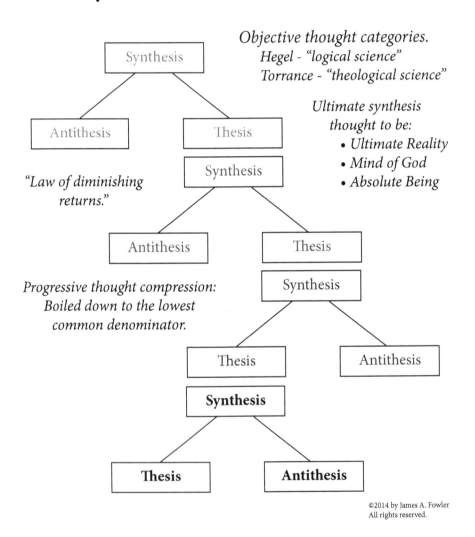

Objective thought categories.
Hegel - "logical science"
Torrance - "theological science"

Ultimate synthesis
thought to be:
- *Ultimate Reality*
- *Mind of God*
- *Absolute Being*

Synthesis

Antithesis   Thesis

Synthesis

"Law of diminishing
returns."

Antithesis   Thesis

Synthesis

Progressive thought compression:
Boiled down to the lowest
common denominator.

Thesis   Antithesis

Synthesis

Thesis   **Antithesis**

Kierkegaard's Inverted Existentialism

Soren Kierkegaard referred to his thinking as an "inverted dialectic"
Inverted • from objective to subjective categories
• from mental ideology to personal & experiential
• from static particulars to dynamic processes

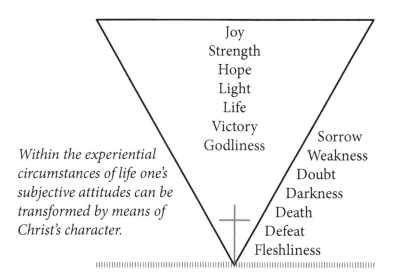

Joy
Strength
Hope
Light
Life
Victory
Godliness

Sorrow
Weakness
Doubt
Darkness
Death
Defeat
Fleshliness

Within the experiential circumstances of life one's subjective attitudes can be transformed by means of Christ's character.

"Truth is Subjectivity"

Interactive Dialectics

God's Self-revelation
Divine Pivot Point

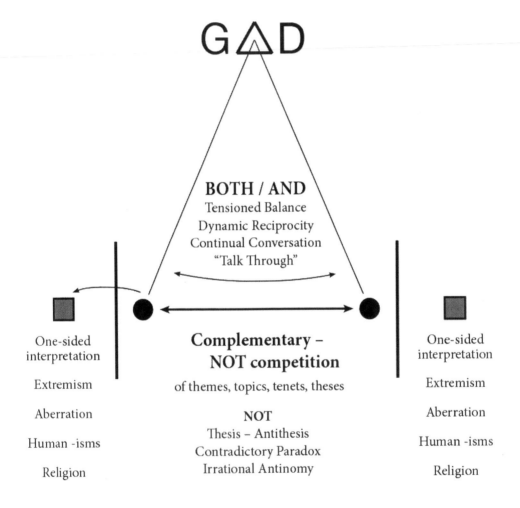

G△D

BOTH / AND
Tensioned Balance
Dynamic Reciprocity
Continual Conversation
"Talk Through"

One-sided
interpretation

Extremism

Aberration

Human -isms

Religion

**Complementary –
NOT competition**

of themes, topics, tenets, theses

NOT
Thesis – Antithesis
Contradictory Paradox
Irrational Antinomy

One-sided
interpretation

Extremism

Aberration

Human -isms

Religion

BOTH / AND
Dialectic Charts

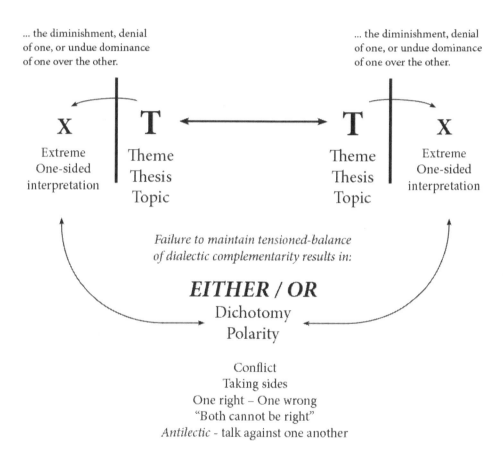

... the diminishment, denial of one, or undue dominance of one over the other.

... the diminishment, denial of one, or undue dominance of one over the other.

X — Extreme One-sided interpretation

T — Theme Thesis Topic

T — Theme Thesis Topic

X — Extreme One-sided interpretation

Failure to maintain tensioned-balance of dialectic complementarity results in:

EITHER / OR
Dichotomy
Polarity

Conflict
Taking sides
One right – One wrong
"Both cannot be right"
Antilectic - talk against one another

AVOIDING THE DITCHES

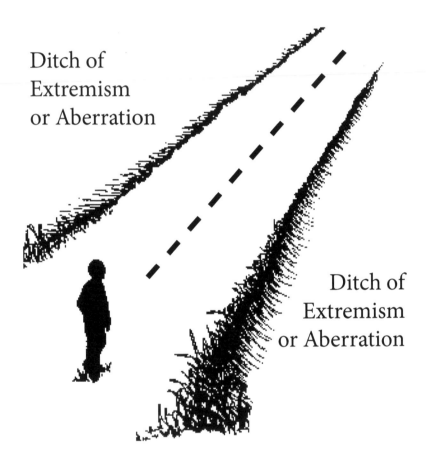

Ditch of
Extremism
or Aberration

Ditch of
Extremism
or Aberration

Illustration by Carrie McDaniels
©2014 by James A. Fowler

202

Philosophical Foundations
of Dialectic Thought

Plato

428–328 B.C.

Aristotle

384–322 B.C.

Approach to knowledge *a priori* Prior to observation speculation - postulation	Approach to knowledge *a posteriori* After observation observation - evaluation
Noumena Conceptual / Mental	Phenomena Perceptual / Experiential
Objectivity External - detachment	Subjectivity Internal - involvement
Ideological dialectics rhetorical, forensic	Syllogistic dialectics If...then...therefore
BEING Essence	**DOING** Function

Philosophical Foundations

Dialectic – Both/And

Extremism

Being

Essence
Reality
Ontological
Conceptual
Thought
Noumena
Rational
Objective
Independent
Transcendent
Universal

Essentialism
Realism
Idealism
Conceptualism
Rationalism
Gnosticism
Rationalism
Objectivism
Absolutism
Deism
Universalism

Extremism

Doing

Function
Activity
Operational
Perceptual
Expression
Phenomena
Experiential
Subjective
Relative
Immanent
Particular

Functionalism
Activism
Dynamism
Visualism
Expressionism
Phenomenalism
Existentialism
Subjectivism
Relativism
Immanentism
Particularism

Bibliography

BIBLIOGRAPHY

Bahm, Archie J., *Polarity, Dialectic and Organicity*.
Albuquerque: World Books. 1976.

Boa, Kenneth, *God, I Don't Understand*. Wheaton: Victor
Books. 1975.

Callen, Barry L., *Caught Between Truths: The Central
Paradoxes of Christian Faith*. Lexington: Emeth Press.
2007.

Crawford, Nathaniel Macon, *Christian Paradoxes*.
Nashville: South-Western Publishing House. 1858.

Crawford, Thomas J., *The Mysteries of Christianity, Being
the Baird Lecture for 1874*. Edinburgh: William
Blackwood & Sons. 1874.

Cumming, Robert Denoon, *Starting Point: An Introduction
to the Dialectic of Existence*. Chicago: The University
of Chicago Press. 1979.

Diem, Hermann, *Kierkegaard's Dialectic of Existence*.
Translated by Harold Knight. Edinburgh/London:
Oliver and Boyd. 1959.

Dunning, Stephen N., *Dialectical Readings: Three Types of
Interpretation*. University Park: The Pennsylvania State
University Press. 1997.

Dunning, Stephen N., *Kierkegaard's Dialectic of
Inwardness: A Structural Analysis of the Theory of
Stages*. Princeton: Princeton University Press. 1985.

Govett, Robert, *The Two-foldness of Divine Truth.*
Hayesville: Schoettle Publishing Co. 2003.

Grounds, Vernon C., "The Postulate of Paradox." Bulletin
of the Evangelical Theological Society 7.1 (Winter
1964). Pgs. 3-21.

Hazelton, Roger, "The Nature of Christian Paradox."
Theology Today. 1949. Pgs. 324-335.

Herbert, R. T., *Paradox and Identity in Theology.* Ithaca:
Cornell University Press. 1979.

Holloway, Richard, *Suffering, Sex and Other Paradoxes.*
Wilton: Morehouse Barlow. 1984.

Kierkegaard, Soren, *Concluding Unscientific Postscript.*
Cambridge: Cambridge University Press. 2009.

Kierkegaard, Soren, *Either/Or* (2 volumes). Garden City:
Anchor Books. 1959.

Kierkegaard, Soren, *Philosophical Fragments.* Princeton:
Princeton University Press. 2013.

Mackenzie, Donald, *Christianity – The Paradox of God.*
The James Sprunt Lectures for 1933. Delivered at
Union Theological Seminary. New York: Fleming H.
Revell Company. 1933.

Mansel, Henry Longueville, *The Limits of Religious
Thought; Examined in Eight Lectures Delivered at
Oxford.* Boston: Gould and Lincoln. 1860.

Mayers, Ronald B., *Both/And: A Balanced Apologetic.*
Chicago: Moody Press. 1984.

Murphree, Jon Tal, *Divine Paradoxes: A Finite View of an Infinite God – A Response to Process and Openness Theologies*. Camp Hill: Christian Publications. 1998.

Nichols, Aidan, *No Bloodless Myth: A Guide Through Balthasar's Dramatics*. Series: Introduction to Hans Urs Von Balthasar. Washington D.C.: Catholic University of America Press. 2000.

Palmer, Parker J., *The Promise of Paradox: A Celebration of Contradictions in the Christian Life*. Notre Dame: Ave Maria Press. 1980.

Parker, Herbert, *Memorials of Godliness and Christianity*. "The Character of a Christian in Paradoxes and Seeming Contradictions." London: By A. M. for T. Underhill. 1655.

Ramsdell, Edward T., *The Christian Perspective*. New York: Abingdon-Cokesbury Press. 1950.

Rose, Tim. *Kierkegaard's Christocentric Theology*. Series: Ashgate New Critical Thinking in Theology and Biblical Studies. Aldershot: Ashgate Publishing. 2001.

Sikes, Walter W., *On Becoming the Truth: An Introduction to the Life and Thought of Soren Kierkegaard*. St. Louis: The Bethany Press. 1968.

Slaatte, Howard A., *The Paradox of Existentialist Theology: The Dialectics of a Faith-Subsumed Reason-in Existence*. New York: Humanities Press. 1971.

Slaatte, Howard A., *The Pertinence of the Paradox: The Dialectics of Reason-in-Existence*. New York: Humanities Press. 1968.

Standish, N. Graham, *Pardoxes for Living: Cultivating Faith in Confusing Times*. Louisville: Westminster, John Knox Press. 2001.

Strawser, Michael, *Both/And: Reading Kierkegaard from Irony to Edification*. New York: Fordham University Press. 1997.

Thomas, J. Heywood, *Subjectivity and Paradox*. Oxford: Basil Blackwell, 1957.

Venning, Ralph, *Orthodox Paradoxes Theoretical and Experimental*. London: Printed for John Hancock, at the three Bibles in Popes Head Alley in Cornhill, 1677.

Von Balthasar, Hans Urs, *Theo-Drama: Vol. 1: Prolegomena*. San Francisco: Ignatius Press. 2013.

Von Balthasar, Hans Urs, *Theo-Drama: Vol. 2: Dramatis Personae: Man in God*. San Francisco: Ignatius Press. 2013.

Von Balthasar, Hans Urs, *Theo-Drama: Vol. 3: Dramatis Personae: Persons in Christ*. San Francisco: Ignatius Press. 2013.

Von Balthasar, Hans Urs, *Theo-Drama: Vol. 4: The Action*. San Francisco: Ignatius Press. 2013.

Von Balthasar, Hans Urs, *Theo-Drama: Vol. 5: Last Act*. San Francisco: Ignatius Press. 2013.

Walsh, Sylvia, *Living Christianly: Kierkegaard's Dialectic of Christian Existence*. University Park: The Pennsylvania State University Press. 2005.

Walsh, Sylvia, *Kierkegaard: Thinking Christianly in an Existential Mode*. Oxford: Oxford University Press. 2009.

67544723R00124

Made in the USA
Middletown, DE
23 March 2018